THE LAND AND PEOPLE OF EGYPT

THE LAND AND PEOPLE

OF

EGYPT

BY

ZAKI NAGUIB MAHMOUD

PORTRAITS OF THE NATIONS SERIES

J. B. Lippincott Company, Philadelphia and New York

TO
Datus C. Smith Jr.
AND
Hassan Galal El Aroussy
without whose encouragement this book
would never have appeared

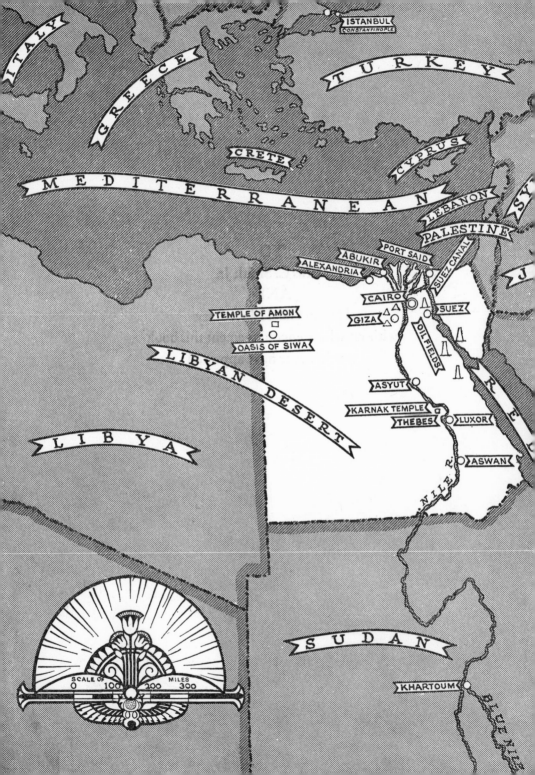

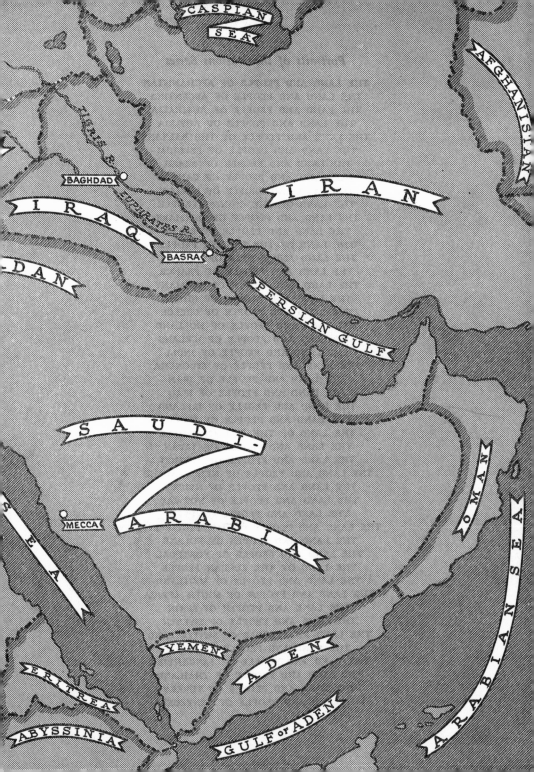

Portraits of the Nations Series

THE LAND AND PEOPLE OF AFGHANISTAN
THE LAND AND PEOPLE OF ARGENTINA
THE LAND AND PEOPLE OF AUSTRALIA
THE LAND AND PEOPLE OF AUSTRIA
THE LAND AND PEOPLE OF THE BALKANS
THE LAND AND PEOPLE OF BELGIUM
THE LAND AND PEOPLE OF BRAZIL
THE LAND AND PEOPLE OF CANADA
THE LAND AND PEOPLE OF CEYLON
THE LAND OF THE CHINESE PEOPLE
THE LAND AND PEOPLE OF DENMARK
THE LAND AND PEOPLE OF EGYPT
THE LAND OF THE ENGLISH PEOPLE
THE LAND AND PEOPLE OF FINLAND
THE LAND AND PEOPLE OF FRANCE
THE LAND AND PEOPLE OF GERMANY
THE LAND AND PEOPLE OF GHANA
THE LAND AND PEOPLE OF GREECE
THE LAND AND PEOPLE OF HOLLAND
THE LAND AND PEOPLE OF ICELAND
THE LAND AND PEOPLE OF INDIA
THE LAND AND PEOPLE OF INDONESIA
THE LAND AND PEOPLE OF IRAN
THE LAND AND PEOPLE OF IRAQ
THE LAND AND PEOPLE OF IRELAND
THE LAND AND PEOPLE OF ISRAEL
THE LAND OF THE ITALIAN PEOPLE
THE LAND AND PEOPLE OF JAPAN
THE LAND AND PEOPLE OF MEXICO
THE LAND AND PEOPLE OF NEW ZEALAND
THE LAND AND PEOPLE OF NIGERIA
THE LAND AND PEOPLE OF NORWAY
THE LAND AND PEOPLE OF PERU
THE LAND AND PEOPLE OF THE PHILIPPINES
THE LAND AND PEOPLE OF POLAND
THE LAND AND PEOPLE OF PORTUGAL
THE LAND OF THE RUSSIAN PEOPLE
THE LAND AND PEOPLE OF SCOTLAND
THE LAND AND PEOPLE OF SOUTH AFRICA
THE LAND AND PEOPLE OF SPAIN
THE LAND AND PEOPLE OF SWEDEN
THE LAND AND PEOPLE OF SWITZERLAND
THE LAND AND PEOPLE OF SYRIA
THE LAND AND PEOPLE OF TANGANYIKA
THE LAND AND PEOPLE OF THAILAND
THE LAND AND PEOPLE OF TURKEY
THE LAND AND PEOPLE OF VENEZUELA

CONTENTS

1. THE GIFT OF THE NILE . page 11

2. THE DAYS OF THE PHARAOHS 20

3. CHRISTIANITY IN EGYPT . . 32

4. WHAT IS ISLAM? 40

5. EGYPT IN HER MIDDLE AGES 49

6. EGYPT IN THE *Arabian Nights* 60

7. A CENTURY OF AWAKENING 65

8. INDEPENDENT EGYPT . . . 75

9. CAIRO AND ALEXANDRIA . . 79

10. AGRICULTURE AND THE COUNTRYSIDE 91

11. MODERN INDUSTRY . . . 101

12. EGYPT COMBATS ILLITERACY 106

13. WOMEN AND THE FAMILY LIFE 112

14. SCIENCE, LITERATURE AND ART 119

1

THE GIFT OF THE NILE

AT THE MEETING POINT OF THE THREE BIG CONTINENTS OF THE ancient world, Europe, Asia and Africa, lies Egypt, or *Misr* as it is called by its own people. Here also two water highways meet, important in the history and commerce of the world: the Mediterranean and the Red Sea, linked by the Suez Canal. The former sea brings Egypt in direct contact with the West, while the latter joins it with the Far East.

This central position between East and West is the clue to Egypt's history and culture. It is not entirely East, nor is it entirely West. It is the combination of both. The two cultures have often met in the land of Egypt. Perhaps the position of the country has made its people able to absorb both outlooks at the same time.

For thousands of years the banks of the Nile have been occupied by the Egyptians. Their character must have been affected by the many changes and many immigrations that have occurred in the long course of time. The Egyptian type, however, has persisted in a strange uniformity. "Egypt is the gift of the Nile," said Herodotus, the ancient Greek historian. And so she truly is. Also true is the fact that the character of its people has been shaped by the river that keeps them alive. The water of the river is, of course, never the same. The Nile is rhythmically emptied and filled anew, year in and year out.

11

Yet the Nile is what it has always been. So are the inhabitants of its valley. Generations come and generations go. Continuous series of changes occur. Yet the Egyptian character remains.

This unchanging individuality may well be the product of the soil. Strangely enough, all the waves of foreign invaders that overran the country at different periods, either kept their original character and, consequently, were soon driven out, or, if they chose to remain, conformed to the national type and were soon absorbed. It is a still stranger fact that even the domestic animals in Egypt are also characterized by uniformity throughout the centuries. Foreign strains of such animals were introduced into the country on certain occasions, but always after a few generations, these were transformed into the Egyptian type of their species. For instance, the ox in the drawings of the ancient temples is exactly the ox which is seen in the fields of present-day Egypt.

Egypt is almost square in shape. On the north is the Mediterranean. On the east the Red Sea. On the west, at the parallel of 24° longitude is Libya. And on the south, at the parallel of 22° latitude is the Sudan. The country is about 380,000 square miles. It is equal in area to the states of California, Arizona and Nevada put together. But of this area only one-thirtieth is inhabited. Twenty-five million people are now squeezed in the valley of the Nile together with the delta—a space equal to only one-half of West Virginia. The inhabited part of Egypt is one of the most densely populated regions in the world.

Through a vast tableland of yellowish-brown dunes and hills, the Nile cuts its course, forming a long and narrow valley with a fan-like delta in the north. On a colored map, the valley with its delta looks like a palm tree, with its tall, slender stem bursting at the top into an umbrella of green leaves. Both the valley and the delta are, perhaps, nowhere excelled in fertility. It is exclusively due to the Nile that such fertility has been forced on the barren desert. The soil is enriched each year by the mud carried down by the river, during the summer, from the highlands of Abyssinia. The Nile flood which is caused by the rains falling on Abyssinia, and which brings the rich soil with it, recurs regularly at the same season of the year.

In June the river slowly begins to rise. At about the middle of July, the increase becomes very rapid. Toward the end of September, the water ceases to rise. It remains at the same level for twenty or thirty days. During the first half of October, it rises again and reaches its highest level. After a while it begins to subside, until it is at its lowest in April and May. The difference between the highest and the lowest states of the river is, on the average, twenty-five feet at Cairo.

The Nile is the world's longest river. The Amazon is second and the Missouri-Mississippi third. In volume, the Nile is surpassed by the Mississippi, the Amazon and Congo. But neither these nor any other river in the world competes with it in historical interest. Its main stream rises south of the equator. It flows down on its way to the Mediterranean in a navigable course, with only few interruptions. Up to the city of Khartoum, the capital of the Sudan, it is called the White Nile. This is because of its clear water. At Khartoum, the Blue Nile—so named because of its dark turbid water—coming down from the heights of Abyssinia, meets the main stream of the river. They meet in the form of an elephant's trunk. Hence comes the name of the city of Khartoum which lies at the meeting point of the two streams. *Khartoum* is the Arabic word for an elephant's trunk. From that point down to the Mediterranean, a distance of 1,350 miles, the Nile runs through barren country. Along the whole of this distance, the river falls 1,240 feet, mainly by six cataracts. Of these cataracts, only one, the farthest to the north, lies in Egypt at the historical city of Aswan.

This great river which has created Egypt, and which keeps it fertile, was a mystery to the ancient inhabitants of the country. They wondered where it obtained its annual and regular rise. Myths were naturally woven around that mystery. It was believed that goddess Isis dropped a tear each year causing the mysterious rise of the Nile. Although the myth has lost its significance in the course of many centuries, people still call the seventeenth night of June (when the river begins to rise), "the night of the drop" without knowing to what drop they refer. The ancient Egyptians even worshiped the Nile, for they were entirely dependent on its blessings for life. They also feared its danger during the period of its rise. When the god-river reached its maximum height, religious celebrations were held in its honor. A beautiful girl is said to have been offered to the Nile each year as a sign of the people's gratitude to the generous god. Even today the rise of the river attracts much attention. People follow the news of its rise and fall in the daily papers, as if they were following the progress of a battle. In August, when the river reaches the height for planting, a public holiday is declared in Cairo, and, in keeping with an old tradition, a formal celebration is held. In such a celebration a doll is thrown into the river instead of the real girl that was formerly offered on such occasion to the god-river.

Egypt is indeed the gift of the Nile in more than one sense. It was the Nile that taught the Egyptians in very early times that there should be law and order in the country. To benefit by the flood, as well as to avoid possible danger that might be caused by it, national unity under a strong central administration had to be achieved. There were later days in the history of Egypt, in the reign of some destructive rulers, when the neglect of the river brought national disaster. Under the rule of such men, famine and starvation frequently came as natural results of neglecting the river flood. The unity of a nation is often brought about by a common interest or the threat of a common enemy; and the Nile was to the Egyptians both a friend and a foe. Is it any wonder, then, that they gathered, even at the dawn of their history, under one banner to enjoy the blessings as well as to avoid the peril of the river?

The great Nile also served as an essential means of communication. The ancient Egyptians made use of the north wind and the south current of the Nile to sail up or down the length of the country. Easy transportation on the Nile made it possible for the builders of the Pyramids and the architects of the huge temples to have stones brought from great distances. Because the river was the nation's chief highway, the Egyptian in earliest times acquired a remarkable ability at shipbuilding. Their ships had oars, masts, sails and cabins. Without the easy navigation of the Nile, commerce could not have flourished to the extent that it did, creating the enormous wealth which made possible the first highly advanced civilization in human history.

In order to make the utmost use of the water of the river, the Egyptians had to develop the art of river engineering and the science of land surveying. In fact, they had to study a variety of sciences related to agriculture. They watched the stars carefully and fixed an exact calendar by which they could foretell the beginning and end of the Nile flood. The yearly overflow of the water wiped out the landmarks that showed which land was whose. It was, therefore, necessary that the land should be measured once every year when the flood subsided. It was also essential that there should be registers in government offices showing the area belonging to each owner. Little wonder that the sacred right of property was among the first moral laws in Egypt.

Without effective laws and a powerful government nothing could have been done to maintain internal peace. As early as the year 3200 B.C., Egypt was a united country under such a government. The king that first achieved the unity of the nation, Mena by name, called himself "King of Upper and Lower Egypt" (i.e. king of the valley and delta). He wore the double crown representing the two parts of the country. It was this king himself who first chose for his capital city of Memphis a site very near that of modern Cairo. He based his choice on the fact that the capital of the two newly combined parts of the country should be at the meeting point of both parts. Such was the big role played by the Nile in creating Egypt.

On both sides of the Nile Valley are deserts: on the east the Arabian, and on the west the Libyan, both of which are utterly waterless. Climatic conditions were different in the very remote past. A few miles east from Cairo there is a petrified forest which is evidence enough that this region, now rainless and barren, must have once been green. The river valley in Egypt is flanked by ranges of hills. The valley differs in width

at different places. It ranges between five and thirty miles.
Both banks are of limestone. From the limestone of the Mokattam hills, which border Cairo on the east side, the buildings of
Cairo are constructed. It was also this material which was used
in building the Pyramids of Giza, across the river.

The vast deserts both to the east and to the west of the Nile
Valley greatly influenced the history of the country. For long
periods of time they served as large buffers that kept the valley
between them almost in complete safety from invasions. This
sheltered position enabled the Egyptians to build up their civilization with all the wonders of art they have left us. Had the
country been exposed to frequent invasions, architects would
have been unable to spend years in building their enormous
monuments.

The stream of life, like the stream of the river itself, went
steadily on in its sheltered valley. Everything in nature emphasized uniformity. Here are the vast deserts on both sides,
changeless. Here is the rhythm of the Nile flood, rising in the
same season, and to the same height year in and year out. To
these steadying factors is to be added the strange uniformity of
weather. With the exception of the delta, which falls within
the region of winter rains, the sky remains continuously blue
and cloudless in the rest of the country all the year round. The
weather in Egypt is not so much a topic of conversation as it is
in other countries. You are almost sure today what it is going
to be like tomorrow or next week.

The Libyan Desert to the west, and the Mediterranean Sea
to the north are the two main factors that influence the climate
of Egypt. During the summer, the hot air of the desert rises
and cool air blows in from the sea. This creates the north wind

that prevails in Egypt. During the rest of the year the wind blows from the west, often changing its course to southwest in the north and northwest in the south. For fifty days in the spring a hot and sandy wind blows from the southwest at irregular intervals for a day or two at a time. This is known by the name of khamsin (from the Arabic word *khamsin* which means fifty). After each khamsin storm the wind changes its direction, and the weather becomes cool and nice, for two or three weeks before another khamsin blows.

In Lower Egypt, which is the northern part of the country, the average temperature is 56° F. in winter and 83° F. in summer. But in Upper Egypt it is different. Whereas the winter temperature in Upper Egypt is nearly the same as it is in Lower Egypt, its summer temperature is much higher. However, the dryness of the Egyptian climate makes its summer heat much less oppressive than lower temperatures in humid countries. Egypt is a perfect winter resort. The summer evenings, no matter how warm it may have been during the day, are invariably cool and pleasant.

Egypt is the gift of the Nile, and so, of course, are the Egyptians. The father of the rivers, as the people call their great Nile, has forced its own qualities on the character of the inhabitants. Between its thin fertile valley and the limitless deserts on both sides, there is but a sharply marked line. From a richly green tract of land, you need only take a step to find yourself in the utterly waterless desert. Life and death in the land of Egypt are close to each other. And so are they in the people's imagination and culture. They think of the afterlife at least as much as they think of the present one. Immortality preoccupies them so much that they have built their monuments to be immortal. Toward those who are too busy with the petty and transient things of this life, they give a sympathetic half-smile, like that on the lips of the Sphinx.

2

THE DAYS OF THE PHARAOHS

I$_T$ IS RATHER DIFFICULT FOR AN AMERICAN READER, WHOSE country is only three centuries old, to grasp the full meaning of sixty centuries, which is the length of Egypt's recorded history.

When Shakespeare wrote his plays—and Shakespeare is but a modern writer—the United States of America did not exist. When Virgil wrote his poetry, Shakespeare's England was not there. When Homer sang his epics, there was no Rome. But when Homer sang his epics in the eleventh century before Christ, thirty centuries had already passed since the Egyptian men of letters started writing their literature. Standing near the Pyramids of Giza, or amidst the temples of Luxor, and fully realizing the length of time that these wonders of architecture have existed, one feels that the greatest and earliest Greek poets and thinkers are but moderns living with us in the same age, if compared to the first builders of the Egyptian civilization.

In the year 3200 B.C., the time at which we first know the Egyptians through their monuments, the development of their civilization had already reached a very high level. As early as that time, they had an elaborate political system, an incredibly advanced art, a fully developed system of writing, a considerable body of literature, a remarkable amount of scientific knowledge, and a sharply outlined religion. How long they had

20

taken to reach such maturity, there is no way of knowing. *maturity*

Time has left many traces during its long march on the land of Egypt. Everywhere in the country there is something which smells of history. Here, near the site of modern Cairo, King Mena first built his capital city of Memphis in 3200 B.C. There, Alexander the Great built Alexandria in 332 B.C. Yonder is the desert monastery of St. Anthony, the first Christian hermit in history.

Traveling along the Nile Valley is traveling along the landmarks of history. The habitable land in Egypt is, indeed, very narrow and limited. But what Egypt lacks in space, it has made up for in time. The United States is the other way round. There is not much density of time in the history of the United States, but this lack has been well made up for by its extensive area. This contrast indicates one of the most important differences between the two countries. Vastness of space begets adventure, while weight of time means a burden of traditions that limit the scope of free movement. In the very old country of Egypt, therefore, people are bound to be conservative, whereas in the very new country of the United States, people are enterprising, with fewer traditions to stop them.

No one civilization can possibly remain unchanged for six thousand years. One source of confusion in people's minds about modern Egypt comes from losing sight of this fact. So many people think of modern Egyptians as if they were still living in the days of the Pyramids and ancient temples. Glorious as Egypt's past was, it is nevertheless a very distant past with many types of civilization. True, many aspects of modern Egyptian life can be traced back across the ages to the time of ancient Egyptians. The farmer today may be using the same plough that his forebears had used. Yet the whole mental setup must necessarily have undergone a radical change.

It is not, then, one civilization that Egypt has passed through in all its history. In fact, it has witnessed three full-fledged civilizations and has embarked on its fourth since the beginning of the last century. These briefly are:

1) The ancient Egyptian civilization which lasted about thirty-five centuries.

2) With the conquest of Egypt by Alexander the Great in the fourth century before Christ, another type of civilization began. This was the Greco-Roman period which lasted for about ten centuries. One can loosely call it the Christian period, as Christianity was the prevailing religion during the latter part of that period.

3) Then came the Arab conquest with its new religion of Islam (Mohammedanism) and its new language, the Arabic language. Since about the middle of the seventh century, Egypt has been chiefly a Moslem and Arabic-speaking country.

4) At the beginning of the nineteenth century, Egypt, although still Moslem and Arabic-speaking, entered on its fourth type of civilization. For the last one and a half centuries, it has been increasingly leaning towards the Western or science-dominated culture.

Of these four phases of Egyptian history, the first was the longest and most characteristic of the nation, because it flowed from within. It is now traditional in writing the history of ancient Egypt, to arrange all the rulers, from Mena, the first king, to Alexander the Great, in thirty-one dynasties; i.e. royal families. For the sake of convenience, these dynasties are again subdivided into kingdoms, each of which assemble a group of successive dynasties with certain similarity among them. Of such kingdoms, or periods, there are three, with an intermediate age of weakness between each two. The Old Kingdom includes the third, fourth, fifth and sixth Dynasties, and lies between 2780 B.C. and 2280 B.C. From the seventh to the tenth Dynasties, 2280 to 2050 B.C., is the so-called First Intermediate Period. The Middle Kingdom is composed of the eleventh and the twelfth Dynasties, from 2134 to 1778 B.C. From the thirteenth to the seventeenth Dynasties is the Second Intermediate Period, during the latter part of which comes the foreign rule of the Hyksos. This period lasted from 1778 to 1567 B.C. Then comes the New Kingdom comprising the eighteenth, nineteenth and twentieth Dynasties, and dating from 1567 to 1090 B.C. A series of royal houses then follows with the historic name of the Late Period, bringing us down to the days of Alexander the Great.

The most important monuments that remain of the Old Kingdom are the Pyramids and the Sphinx. There are five groups of Pyramids, all of which are more or less in the neighborhood of the ancient capital city of Memphis, a few miles from the site of modern Cairo. Of those groups the Pyramids of Giza are most famous. These huge constructions show, among other things, how wealthy the nation, and how strong the central government must have been. The enormous amount of labor necessary for the building of the Great Pyramid of Cheops (called Khufu by the Egyptians) may be approximately imagined if the reader realizes how colossal this monument is. Many a building in the world cannot be rightly estimated in size unless closely seen. This writer was never fully aware of the size of the Statue of Liberty near New York, or the Washington Memorial in Washington, D.C., until he climbed up to their tops. Such is the case, on a larger scale, with the Great Pyramid of Giza. It is built of about 2,300,000 blocks of stone, some of which weigh 150 tons each. About 100,000 men were employed for twenty years in building it. The technique of work is best described by Herodotus in the following passage, "This pyramid was first built in the form of a flight of steps. After the workmen had completed the pyramid in this form, they raised the other stones by means of machines made of short beams, from the ground of the first tier of steps; and after the stone was placed there it was raised to the second tier by another machine; for there were as many machines as there were tiers of steps; or perhaps the same machine, if it was easily moved, was raised from one tier to the other, as it was required for lifting the stones. The highest part of the pyramid was thus finished first, the parts adjoining it were taken next, and the lowest part, next to the earth, was completed last."

The great pyramid covers an area of more than half a million square feet. Time has eroded much of its sides. It is much less in size now than it was. In its present state, the length of each side is 750 feet. The height is 451 feet.

Ancient Egyptians believed in the immortality of the human soul. Since the natural dwelling place of a soul was its body, it was desirable that that body should be preserved. These enormous pyramids were built to serve as tombs for the kings' bodies after death. They were all built on the western bank of the Nile, for the west, where the sun disappeared, indicated the end of the worldly life.

Everything possible was done inside the royal tomb for the preservation of life in the second world. The body was embalmed against destruction. Necessary belongings were placed with the dead body ready for use if needed. If it was impossible to place certain things that might be needed, these were painted or engraved on the walls, in the belief that the drawings would be turned magically into real things at the right moment. This strange idea proved to be fruitful in creating art. Artists did their best to draw, engrave or carve all sorts of things. First-class work representing a large variety of things is still to be seen clearly on the walls of the ancient tombs: field ploughing, crop harvesting, bread baking, cattle grazing, tables with meals fully prepared. If we are no more interested in their beliefs, we can still enjoy the enormous wealth of art which resulted from those beliefs. One does not need to be Roman Catholic to enjoy the art in a cathedral.

On the same spot where the Pyramids of Giza stand, is the famous Sphinx. Like the great pyramid, it is much more colossal than one might think. It is sixty-six feet high. The ear is four and one-half feet, and the nose is five feet, seven inches. Standing on the upper part of the ear, one cannot stretch one's hand as far as the crown of the head. As is well-known, the Sphinx has the shape of a sitting lion with a human head, and was so shaped to symbolize the combination of power and wisdom—two qualities that were supposed to distinguish the king, or, rather the whole nation.

After an intermediate period of weakness, Egypt jumped again to prosperity and power with the rise of the Middle

Kingdom (2134-1778 B.C.). Eminent among the rulers of that period was Senusert III, about whom many legends were narrated by Greek historians. On his visit to Egypt, Herodotus learned that Senusert III had taken his fleet into the Red Sea and sailed around Africa. When he returned home, he led his army and conquered a large part of the then-known world.

Fragments from the libraries of those times—the oldest libraries in the world—have remained to our day. In these rolls of papyrus we read fascinating stories of adventures in Asia, and a wonderful story of shipwreck at the gate of the unknown ocean. The writer of this story was an Egyptian Ulysses or Sindbad telling about his wanderings in the seas.

One marvels how, at such an early date, the people of Egypt could dig a canal from the north end of the Red Sea westward to the Nile, thus joining the Red Sea with the Mediterranean —a predecessor of the Suez Canal four thousand years ago.

But again Egypt fell into weakness for some time, during which the country was invaded by nomadic people from Asia called the Hyksos. The coming of Joseph to Egypt is said to have occurred in the Hyksos days. It was those nomads who brought horses for the first time into the country.

The driving out of those nomadic invaders was the beginning of the New Kingdom, or the Empire (1567-1090 B.C.). Egypt during this period reached its highest peak of glory. The capital city was the famous Thebes (modern Luxor). The magnificent monuments that cover a large area on both sides of the Nile speak highly of Egypt's power and ability in the days of the Empire.

The Karnak temple on the site of ancient Thebes is one of the wonders in the world of art. A distinguished American historian, James Henry Breasted, describing his visit to Karnak temple, says that it contains the greatest colonnaded hall ever erected by man. The columns of the central aisle are sixty-nine feet high. The vast capital forming the summit of *each* column is large enough to contain a group of a hundred men standing crowded upon it at the same time. The temple rose among towering obelisks and colossal statues of the Pharaohs. The whole was bright with color, flashing at many a point with gold and silver.

The sculptor and the painter added their masterpieces to the grandeur of architecture. The colonnades, with flower capitals, were colored to suggest the plant they represented. About the towering portrait statues set up before the temples of Thebes, the American historian, Breasted, goes on to say: "The sculptors could cut these colossal figures from a single block, although they were sometimes eighty or ninety feet high and weighed as much as a thousand tons. This is a burden equal to the load drawn by a modern freight train, but unlike the trainload it was not cut up into small units of light weight, convenient for handling and loading. Nevertheless, the engineers of the Empire moved many such vast figures for hundreds of miles."

Many a brilliant name in history shone in the time of the New Kingdom. Thutmose III who was the Napoleon of Egypt and its greatest conqueror; Queen Hatshepsut, the first great woman in history; Akhenaton, the first believer in one God, and his Queen Nefertiti; his successor and son-in-law, Tutankhamoun, in whose tomb were found wonders of craftsmanship; Ramses II whose name is usually connected with the exodus of the Hebrews from Egypt—to mention only a few names.

A great event in the history of religion occurred when King Akhenaton (or Ikhnaton) attempted to destroy the old gods of Egypt and to persuade his people to worship one God. He was the first in history to believe in God, using the word "God" in almost exactly the same sense as the Judaic, Christian and Islamic religions use it. In order that the people might forget the old gods, he closed all the temples and turned out their priests. The prophet-king composed his own hymns for his God who was the creator of all races of men, both Egyptians and foreigners. What is more, Akhenaton believed that his God had the nature of a kindly Father, who looked after his creatures. He tells us in one of his beautiful hymns that even the birds in their marshes were aware of His kindness, and raised their wings like arms to praise Him. His hymns were the source of some parts of the Psalms. The following is his famous hymn to Aton which is similar in idea to parts of Psalm 104:

> When thou settest in the western horizon of Heaven,
> The world is in darkness like the dead.
> Men sleep in their chambers, their heads are wrapt up,
> Every lion cometh forth from his den.
> The serpents, they sting.
> Darkness reigns, the world is in silence.
> He that made them has gone to rest in his horizon.
>
> Thou art he who created the man-child in woman,
> Who givest life to the son in the body of his mother,
> Who soothest him that he may not weep,
> A nurse even in the womb.

The peace-loving, God-worshiping Akhenaton was too much absorbed in his new faith to keep his country strong. Egypt in his reign looked an easy prey for the enemy. And the people of the country themselves turned away from him. The common people never learned to accept the new religion. The discarded priests were resentful of the closing of their temples and the loss of their power. Hopeless of getting the world, inside the country and outside, to accept his new beliefs, Akhenaton died, leaving Egypt on the path to downfall.

No longer was Egypt the great power she had been. She fell into a period of weakness and was exposed to many invasions from abroad. Yet there were brilliant names that shone through the prevailing darkness. Worthiest of all was King Necho (610-594 B.C.) who sent a fleet all around Africa. The sea-loving king was eager to connect the Mediterranean with the Red Sea by means of a canal. The scheme was more than half completed when a divine oracle ordered that the work should be stopped at once, as it was against the interests of the country. It was one hundred years later, when the Persians conquered Egypt, that Darius (521-486 B.C.) completed the canal so that Egyptian products might be shipped easily to Persia.

Those were the days of the Pharaohs. One cannot be too proud of their legacy. Look at the enormous wealth they have contributed to human civilization. They gave the world the first highly developed practical arts, like metalwork, weaving, glass-making, paper-making, and many others. They built the earliest sea-going ships. They gave us the earliest alphabet for writing. They composed the earliest known tales, poems and drama. They gave us the calendar. They took the first long stride in mathematics, astronomy and medicine. They were the first people to establish an elaborate system of government, a government for their single nation, as well as a government to rule an empire composed of a number of nations.

And above all they gave us art. In architecture, sculpture, mural-painting, Egypt reached a summit surpassed by none in the ancient world, not excluding Greece. Champollion, the famous French scholar who deciphered the writings of the ancient Egyptians, said, "No people, ancient or modern, have had such sublime and vast conception of the art of building as the Egyptians. Their vision is that of men a hundred feet high."

It would be a mistake to apply the criteria of the classical art of Europe to the art of the Egyptians. They worked on different principles, and they should be judged by those principles. For instance, an Egyptian painter used two-dimensional drawings, unlike the three-dimensional classical paintings of Europe and America, but very much like the work of the modern school of art. The Egyptian artist, again, was interested in the form of what he represented in his art, rather than in the imitation of nature. As a result of such principles, you might think that their drawing of a man, say, is distorted, with the feet going sideways while the chest is directed to the front. The head may be painted in profile, while the whole eye is shown on the side. All such things, of course, break the rules of perspective. But the Egyptian artist, very much like the modern artist, was not after the perspective. He was interested in the full form of the thing painted. The form of the foot is better shown when it steps sideways. The form of the chest is better shown when it looks to the front. The profile of the head brings out its form well. The eye must be fully drawn for its form to appear. Why not combine all these parts in such positions, whether or not the final picture represented the body as it is seen? The artist is not a camera. It is not his job to copy nature. Rather, he creates. Such was the conception of the Egyptian artists, and such is also the conception of the ultra-moderns.

The ancient Egyptian artist had a wider understanding of the scope of life than even the Greeks and Romans. Gods, kings, noblemen and priests he, of course, portrayed. But he was no less eager to include in his art every possible thing in the living world. He painted peasants, carpenters, bricklayers; he portrayed children playing, women going to the fields. He produced a rich assortment of animals, reptiles and insects. He even invented combinations in which men and beasts were mixed up together. All aspects of life are represented by the Egyptian artist: farming, cooking, shipbuilding, processions, festivals and thousands of other things. There was nothing in life considered too trivial for the artist to work upon. The mural paintings on the walls of the temples team with pictures of the people and their life. Where else in the world is such a representative gallery of art? It is indeed a great legacy, the legacy of the ancient Egyptians.

3

CHRISTIANITY IN EGYPT

IT WAS IN THE YEAR 332 B.C. THAT ALEXANDER THE GREAT TOOK possession of Egypt. This was the beginning of a new civilization. It was the beginning of the Greco-Roman period, during which Christianity was born. Alexander's campaign was indeed an epoch-making event in the history of the world. Together with the military conquest went a cultural invasion that was the first attempt towards mixing the East with the West in one civilization. The attempt was successful so far as Egypt was concerned. Between Egypt and ancient Greece there was a cultural interrelation of give and take. By a very natural shift, the seat of world culture moved from Athens to Alexandria, the city founded on the Mediterranean by the young hero Alexander.

During his campaign in Egypt, Alexander passed through the Oasis of Siwa, right in the heart of the Libyan Desert, where the temple of Amon was. He was so impressed by the religion of Egypt that he declared himself a worshiper of Amon, and was hailed by the priests as Amon's son. On his deathbed his thoughts were driven only to the Oasis of Siwa, and his last wish was that he should be buried by the side of his "father's temple." But Ptolemy I, who was among Alexander's generals, and who ruled Egypt after him, preferred to bury his master in Alexandria, where his body is still said to be lying.

There followed a ruling family of Ptolemies, under whom the lower valley of the Nile became once more, for three centuries, the seat of a brilliant kingdom. When Rome under Julius Caesar was the leading world power, Cleopatra was the queen of Egypt. It is truly said that Rome which feared nothing else, did fear two people: Hannibal and Cleopatra. She bravely defended her land against the Romans, but lost the battle. In the year 30 B.C., Egypt belonged to Rome.

With the Roman rule came poverty to Egypt. The Romans, unlike the Greeks who had preceded them, were from first to last despised and hated, and feared. In the midst of Egypt's misery under the Romans, there was born in Palestine a child who was to bring a new religion of peace and love to the world. Egyptians were among the first to take interest in the new faith which brought them consolation in their desperate state.

How strange that within less than half a century, Egypt received two visitors who were to change the course of history all the world over, but in quite different ways. Between 30 B.C. and A.D. 10 there came to Egypt Caesar and Christ.

Joseph, Mary and the Child are said to have come from Bethlehem into Egypt, where they settled at a place called Babylon, now a ruined fortress in the southern part of Cairo. In almost every place along their journey, we are told by ancient legends about miracles of healing achieved by the Infant's touch. The idols of the temple of Heliopolis are said to have fallen when the Child was brought into the temple. At a suburb called Matarieh, in the northern part of Cairo, there is still a spring of pure water, in which, we are told, Mary washed her Infant's clothes as they stopped by the side of the road to rest for a while on the last day of their journey. There is also on the same spot an old tree under which they are said to have rested. The Holy Family is believed to have stayed in a house in the part of Cairo called Babylon (not to be confused with the city of Babylon in Asia) where a very old church now stands. This church was built—so the tradition goes—in the Age of Apostles, just on the spot where the Holy Family stayed. It may be the oldest church in the world. The period of the Holy Family's stay in Egypt is differently estimated. Some make it six months. Others extend it from two to four or even six years.

St. Mark is the founder of the Church of Egypt. He belonged to a wealthy family, which was ruined by a nomadic invasion. His father settled near Jerusalem. Peter was connected with the family by marriage, and it was Peter who instructed Mark in Christianity at an early age. Mark's first visit to Egypt was in the year A.D. 45, on which journey he may have been accompanied by St. Peter. When we are told that he was accompanied as far as Babylon by St. Peter, we don't really know which of the two Babylons is meant. Is it the Babylon of Cairo or the Babylon of Asia? It is very likely that Mark and Peter stayed at Babylon in Egypt for some time during which a big part of the Gospel of St. Mark was written.

However, St. Mark settled in Alexandria and started his preaching of Christianity. The first church in Alexandria was built in his time. On the twenty-fifth of April, in the year A.D. 62, which was a Sunday, there was to be a feast celebrated by the Roman pagans. St. Mark denounced the celebration publicly as impious, thus preventing the Christians from taking part in it. There was a riot in the streets of Alexandria. St. Mark was arrested by the Pagans, and dragged by a rope tied around his neck along the main streets of the city. At night he was thrown into prison. On the following day he was dragged to death in the streets. He was buried in the church he had built. For centuries, it was the tradition that the Patriarch of Alexandria should be elected at St. Mark's tomb. St. Mark's body is said to have been removed later to Rome.

In those very early days of the Egyptian Church, many customs were adopted from the ancient Egyptians; some of which still survive in the churches of the West. To mention one thing—wedding rings. The ancient Egyptians, before using coins, used rings of different metals for money. It was the custom that the bridegroom should give his bride a gold ring as a symbol of marriage, and a sign that he thereby gave her his wealth. This custom survived among Egyptians after their conversion to Christianity, and passed from them to the Church all over the world.

Christianity spread rapidly among the people of Egypt. The Roman authorities were so disturbed that they issued a law in the year 204 prohibiting the Roman subjects from embracing the new faith. Not only were there many Christian communities among the people at that time, but also schools of Christian theology flourished in the cultural climate of Alexandria. Worthy of a special note among the early Fathers of the Christian Church is Origen (185-254).

At the age of fifteen, Origen had already distinguished himself in the Christian school of Alexandria. And at that age his father was arrested by the authorities, beheaded, and his property was confiscated. Origen, being the eldest son, was left penniless with a mother to support, and six younger brothers to bring up. Nevertheless, the boy boldly met the situation, and went on, even more enthusiastically, in his religious studies and services. It was a time of fear and trouble in Alexandria. The members of the schools where the new faith was taught ceased to meet in the school buildings. But gradually the young man, Origen, gathered them all around him, thus making himself an easy target for the pagan population and their rulers.

One day, the mob forced him to take part in a pagan festival. They clothed him in the white robes of their priests, and brought him up the steps of the temple. They ordered him to distribute certain palms to the crowd of idol-worshipers who were roaring with laughter below. To answer their silly joke, Origen offered the palm branches to the people as he was commanded to do, but shouted aloud, "Come and receive the palms, not of idols, but of the Lord Jesus Christ."

Typical of an Egyptian saint, Origen was once seized with the passion of self-denial. He fulfilled literally every precept in the New Testament. He refused to own two garments and went barefoot winter and summer. He allowed himself not more than the minimum of the simplest food. It was only his real genius that prevented him from retiring, as fellow saints in those days sometimes did, to a desert cave where he would live and die leaving no trace behind him.

Among the most eminent figures of early Christianity was the world-famous St. Anthony. He was born in Upper Egypt of wealthy Christian parents (about the year 250). Both his parents died when he was eighteen, and left him only a younger sister. Six months after his parents' death, Anthony heard the preacher in the church reciting Christ's address to the rich young man: "If thou wilt be perfect, go and sell all that thou hast, and distribute unto the poor, and thou shalt have treasure in heaven: and come, follow me." Anthony felt as if he were meant personally. He instantly obeyed the order to the letter; keeping only a small part of his money for his sister. But again he soon heard in the church the following command: "Take no thought for the morrow." Then he felt ashamed of himself that he had thought of his sister's future. He sold all his land for the sake of the poor, left his sister under the care of an old woman in the village, and wandered away. From that moment onward, his sole purpose was to fight in himself the desires of the flesh. After much wandering far afield, barefoot and alone, he finally shut himself up in a ruined building on the bank of the Nile. He declined to meet any human being. However the man was soon known among the people as a blessed saint. The simple peasants gathered from all places to listen to what the invisible hermit might say. From inside his building, still unseen by the gathered crowd, Anthony would address the people in utterances highly charged with emotion. His admirers brought him a sufficient amount of bread of a kind that would keep for months. Egyptian farm laborers, even today, still use, when necessary, that kind of bread. It becomes so hard that it has to be moistened with water before it can be eaten. For twenty years Anthony lived in his retreat, unseen but with a rapidly growing fame. This kind of life, of course, gave rise to a thousand legends that still stick to his name.

In the latter part of his life, however, Anthony moved to a mountainous region between the Red Sea and the Nile, where he changed his mode of life. The monastery of St. Anthony still stands on that spot. In order to save his disciples the trouble of coming a long distance to bring him food, he cultivated a little piece of land to supply himself with his needs. He also kept himself busy making mats. Besides, he preached to the disciples who soon gathered around him. He had no books, but he seems to have thought deeply and taught well. He was now so much interested in the outer world that he wrote his advice more than once to people in authority, who, he thought, needed guidance.

In due time all Egypt turned Christian, and so she remained until the seventh century, when the Arabs, who had just adopted the new religion of Islam, conquered Egypt in the year 640. Gradually, the Egyptians were converted to the new faith and began to use the Arabic language. Christians in Egypt today form a small minority. The proportion of Christians to Moslems is about one to ten.

The Egyptian Christians are known as Copts, and their church as the Coptic Church. The word "Copt" is the corruption of the Greek name of Egypt. For an Egyptian Moslem, there is always the possibility that he may be the descendant of the conquering Arabs. But for a Copt there is no such possibility. Copts, therefore, may be taken with certainty as the real descendants of ancient Egyptians. The Coptic Patriarch is elected by the Copts themselves.

Most of the Egyptian Copts are Orthodox. The rest are either Protestants, recently converted, or Roman Catholics. The Gospels are translated into Arabic and are available everywhere at low prices. Discrimination on any basis is entirely absent from the land of Egypt. Unless it were pointed out who was Moslem and who was Christian, one would never know who was what. One must remember that Christianity and Islam are more alike than different. As we shall see in the next chapter, a Moslem is required to believe in Christ and the Bible, which brings him very close to his Christian fellow citizen. Furthermore, the long history of the Egyptians has taught them to stand shoulder to shoulder as one united nation, no matter what differences there may be among the individual citizens.

4

WHAT IS ISLAM?

"ISLAM" IS THE RIGHT WORD FOR SO-CALLED MOHAMMEDAN-ism. It is the name of the religious faith preached by Moham-med in the first half of the seventh century. The adherents of Islam are called Moslems. "Islam" is an Arabic word which means the surrender of one's will to the will of God. A Mos-lem, therefore, is a person who so submits himself to the divine Will. The vast majority of Egyptians, indeed the vast major-ity of the people of the Middle East, are Moslems.

The prophet of Islam was Mohammed. He was born in the year A.D. 570. His father died shortly before his birth. When he was six, his mother also died. The orphan was brought up by his uncle. He was a citizen of Mecca which was at the time a commercial center. In due time, Mohammed himself took part in business.

When he was forty years old, Mohammed's ministry began. The message was chiefly meant for the idol-worshipers in Ara-bia. Such idolatry was by no means uncommon in the Proph-et's homeland.

The Koran is the sacred book of the Moslems. The word "Koran" is an Arabic word which means "recital." The Mos-lems believe that the verses of the Koran were divinely in-spired, not all at once, but in sections and on appropriate occasions. Each verse or group of verses was sent in relation

40

to the happenings of the moment. These inspired utterances were revealed to the Prophet at two different places, and in two different conditions. The first part was revealed to him when he was still at Mecca, strongly opposed by his fellow citizens. The latter part was sent at Medina, where he had migrated, and from where he finally succeeded in getting his message heard and believed in. His migration from Mecca to Medina (A.D. 622) was later taken as a starting date for the Arabic calendar.

A few years after Mohammed's death (A.D. 633) the verses of the Koran were compiled from the various materials on which they had been recorded during the Prophet's life. Together with these written records, quite a few of the companions of the Prophet had learned the whole lot by heart. The complied verses were classified into one hundred and fourteen divisions, arranged roughly according to length, the longest first.

The koranic verses were so beautifully written that in the Prophet's time, and ever since they were too beautiful for imitation. Among the Arabic men of letters, Moslems or otherwise, there is a consensus of opinion that the koranic literary style has brought the genius of the Arabic language to its height. The Koran, when translated to a non-Arabic language, necessarily loses a great deal of its literary value. George Sale (1697-1736), one of the translators of the Koran into English, warns his reader that he ". . . must not imagine the translation to come up to the original, notwithstanding my endeavours to do it justice."

First and foremost among the principles of Islam is the belief in one God. The Arabic word for God is Allah—a word composed of two parts: (1) Al = the; and (2) Ilah = God. The word Allah, therefore, literally means "the God." It will be observed that this same Arabic word Allah is the one used by both Christians and Jews who speak the Arabic language. The French word for God is Dieu, the Arabic word is Allah, but the meaning of all these words is the same. This is emphasized because many people are misled by the difference in words into the belief that Moslems do not worship God as do other religions.

Judaism, Christianity and Islam all appeared in the Middle East. They all preached the belief in God, with the following differences. Mohammed, like Hebrew prophets, believed in one God. But, unlike those prophets, he conceived of Him, not as a tribal God concerned only with a chosen people, but as a universal God for all. Christianity, of course, thought of Him as a universal God, too. But, unlike Christianity, Islam rejected the plurality involved in the doctrine of the Trinity. In other words, from Judaism, Islam took the unity of God. From Christianity it took His universality. Hence came the belief of Moslems in one God for all.

Together with the belief in the absolute unity of God goes the belief in the prophets and apostles formerly sent by Him. It is worth particular mentioning that Moslems, accordingly, believe in Moses and Christ and in their divine messages. In this light we may be able to understand what Mohammed meant by admitting that the Scripture given to him was but a restatement of the true doctrine revealed to the prophets and apostles before him.

Strange enough, while the Koran stresses time and again the supernatural aspects of Jesus Christ, it denies anything superhuman about Mohammed. He is but a mortal man. Like other men he was born, and like other men he would die. Furthermore, he was given no miraculous powers. Asked by his fellow citizens to show them a miracle that would prove his right to claim the gift of prophecy, he self-confidently appealed to the Koran itself.

According to Islam, an individual human being is taken to be originally sinless, and thus morally responsible. God has given each and every man the power of self-government. Yes, everything was predestined by the divine Will. But the freedom of the human will was among those predestined principles. Hence came man's entire responsibility for his voluntary actions. Moslems believe in the Day of Judgment, when men's actions shall be weighed. Reward or punishment shall be estimated accordingly.

Such moral responsibility based on the individual's freedom to act rightly or wrongly, leads to the consequence that there is no need of clergy mediating between man and God. That every individual soul must seek his own salvation is one of the cornerstones of Islam. In Islam no priests are needed. So-called "men of religion" in Islam are simply those who choose to devote their studies mostly to theology. But such men are not considered any closer to God than others. Islam teaches that on the goodness of action alone are the values of people to be estimated.

It is difficult to see whence came the accusation that Islam was intolerant and propagated by the sword. The Koran states clearly that "There should be no compulsion in religion." The Prophet of Islam was ordered therein: "Fight in defence of the cause of God against those who attack you, but begin no hostilities. Truly, God loveth not the aggressors. And if they [the enemies of Islam] incline towards peace, incline thou also to peace." Among the teachings of the Koran in this respect are the following: "Live peacefully with one another" and "Repel the evil deed which is vain and frivolous with such a better answer as would make [the aggressor] feel as though he was a good friend."

One of the chief rituals of Islam is the observance of prayers at five fixed times of day: at daybreak; at midday; in the afternoon; at sunset and at nightfall. Each of these prayers consists of a certain number of bowings accompanied by certain words. The words "Allahu Akbar" (God is most Great) is repeated throughout the performance. This important phrase is not without a far-reaching significance. If it were always kept in mind, no tyrant, indeed no difficulty whatsoever might frighten the true believer. For whatever seems great, one should remember that God is still greater.

Prayers may be performed anywhere, but preferably at a mosque in a congregation. They are called for by a muezzin (a caller for prayer), whose sonorous call takes the place of bells. An English traveler, one hundred years ago, wrote the following passage to describe the effect of the muezzin's calls breaking the silence of the night. Cairo now, of course, is a hundred times busier than what it was in the days of that traveler's visit. The description, however, still holds true in some smaller provincial cities. Said the writer: "[at dawn] the musical chant of the Muezzens from the thousand minarets of Cairo sounds most impressively through the clear and silent air. The voices of the criers thus raised above the city always struck me as having a holy and beautiful effect. First one or two are heard faintly in the distance, then one close to you, then the cry is taken up from the minarets of other mosques, and at last, from one end of the town to the other, the measured chant falls pleasingly on the ear, inviting the faithful to prayer. For a time it seems as if there was a chorus of voices in the air, like spirits, calling upon each other to worship the creator of all things. Soon the sound dies away, there is a silence for a while, and then commence the hum and bustle of the awakening city. This cry of man, to call his brother man to prayer, seems to me more appropriate and more accordant to religious feeling than the clang and jingle of European bells." Ablution, washing before prayer, is a necessary ritual. It was, of course, meant as a sanitary measure. During prayers a worshiper turns his face toward Mecca, as the Jews and some of the Christian sects turn toward Jerusalem or toward the east. On Fridays the midday prayer is usually done at the mosque and is preceded by a sermon.

The giving of alms to the needy is another main principle of Islam. It is a religious duty that the financially able should help the poor in a systematic way. A certain percentage of the rich person's property is due annually to the poverty-stricken. A number of conditions are stipulated for the performance by the rich of this duty. It is provided, for instance, that the property subject to this duty should have been owned for the whole past year, and that the owner should be free from debts. The property referred to should not include the necessities of one's life such as his dwelling, his furniture or his clothing. Productive implements and scholarly books and apparatus are also exempted.

This alms is not to be confused with the tax due to the State.

The alms, unlike the tax, is to be voluntarily given, not levied by the Government. This giving of alms to those who need it is almost invariably mentioned, in the Koran, with the observance of prayer. The two principles seem to go together, the one as an inward sign of piety, and the other as an outward sign.

Another Islamic ritual is the observance of fasting during the month of Ramadan, the ninth month in the Arabic calendar. The months of this calendar are lunar, that is, each month begins with the appearance of the new moon and starts from the historical event of Mohammed's migration from Mecca to Medina in the fall of the year A.D. 622. Fasting, in the sense of abstinence from one thing or another, seems to be an essential part of most religions. Abstaining voluntarily from the natural desires of the flesh is self-discipline. The essence of morality, in fact, is self-control or self-government; and fasting in all its senses is an effective educational tool towards such a moral end.

During the month of Ramadan, a Moslem's religious duty is to abstain completely from food and drink during the hours of daylight, or more strictly from dawn to sunset. Social life has a peculiar color during this month. Fasting does not enable people to carry out their normal activities by day with their usual vigor. Everything slows down during the day-time hours. At sunset the streets are empty. Everybody is at home to break his day's fast just at the moment of sundown. Shortly after, the streets begin to be crowded again. Cafés and similar public places are full of people till the late hours of the night. Mosques are unusually filled with worshipers. Groups of children are to be seen everywhere, each carrying a lantern with colored glass, chanting certain phrases. They knock at doors for sweets, just as American children do on Halloween. Shortly before dawn, a stir is to be heard in the houses. People rise at this early hour to eat, preparing themselves for another day of fasting. The eve of the twenty-seventh day of Ramadan is considered especially holy, for it is believed that the Koran was first sent down to Mohammed on this night. Prayers are best listened to on this holy occasion, and blessings are more likely to descend from heaven on the pious. On the three days following the end of Ramadan, Moslems celebrate what is called "the lesser feast." They rejoice at the termination of the fasting. And like Christmas with Christians, parents give presents to their children.

A pilgrimage to Mecca once in one's life is another duty of a Moslem if he can afford it. If the congregational prayers at the Mosque are considered as a social tie in each locality, the wider gathering of pilgrims from all parts of the world is certainly a means to creating a kind of international brotherhood. The occasion takes place ten weeks after the end of the fasting month. On approaching Mecca, a pilgrim replaces his clothes with a simple piece of cloth. By this he symbolizes the removal of all social differences which may be shown by normal clothes. All now are entirely equal. The pilgrims then carry out certain traditional ceremonies, concluding their pilgrimage with each of them sacrificing a sheep in memory of the sacrifice of Abraham of his son Ismail. It is worth mentioning here that Islam claimed to be fundamentally, not a new religion, but a revival of the pure faith of Abraham. Judaism was the religion of Moses, and Christianity was that of Jesus. But before both was Abraham with a pure and simple faith of one absolute

God; and on the Abrahamic belief Islam is based. On the same day of the pilgrimage ceremonies, all Moslems, wherever they are, celebrate what is called "the greater feast." Every Moslem, if financially able, sacrifices a sheep on this day. Meat is given by the rich to the poor, as a result, everyone, rich and poor, eats meat on that occasion.

Together with these principles and rituals of Islam, there is a complete legal code and a full system of morality.

The minaret of Iman El Shafei Mosque, Cairo

The sheep way at Luxor

An obelisk

The sea front in Alexandria

The mosques of Sultan Hassan and Al Rifaii, Cairo

The Sphinx at Giza

The Pyramids at Giza

Boats on the Nile River, Cairo

Ancient colonnade at Karnak

The State Building in Cairo

Aerial view of the Nile at Cairo

A beach at Alexandria

The Temple of Luxor

University of Cairo

A laboratory in the School of Science, University of Cairo

An Egyptian brass engraver at Khan el Khalili Bazaar, Cairo

5

EGYPT IN HER MIDDLE AGES

IN THE YEAR A.D. 640 A SMALL ARMY OF MOSLEM ARABS, FILLED
with enthusiasm for the new faith, Islam, conquered Egypt.
Since then Egypt has been a Moslem country, and the Egyptians have been an Arabic-speaking people. But although Islam
has remained the prevailing religion in Egypt to the present
day, yet the historically technical term "Moslem Egypt" applies only to the period extending from the Arab conquest of
the country in the seventh century, down to the French campaign in Egypt, led by Napoleon in 1798. There is reason
enough for this distinction. The thoroughly Islamic civilization which dominated Egypt for twelve centuries—from the
seventh century to the beginning of the nineteenth century—
has given way to so-called Western civilization. During the
twelve centuries of the Moslem period, Egypt had been almost
exclusively facing East, turning its back to the Mediterranean
and, consequently, to the West. But since the beginning of the
nineteenth century, it has gradually changed its point of view,
and has increasingly been absorbing the cultural elements of
the West.

During centuries from the seventh to the nineteenth,
Egypt was governed by a series of ruling houses; some of these
houses were under the authority of the central government of
the Caliph in Baghdad, some were independent. Among the

independent ruling families were the Fatimids who established their authority in 969. They are important first, because they founded the capital city of Al-Qahira (i.e. Cairo). Memphis, the oldest capital city of ancient Egypt, was but a few miles from the site of Cairo. But what is now Cairo was the choice of the Fatimids.

The name Al-Qahira is an Arabic word meaning triumphant. The story goes that when Gawhar, the general of the Fatimid army, captured the site of Cairo, he at once laid the foundations of a new city, the would-be capital of the country. At a distance of about a mile from the river, he marked out the boundaries. A square, somewhat less than a mile each way, was pegged out with poles, and astrologers consulted together to determine the right moment for the opening ceremony. Bells were hung on ropes from pole to pole, and at the signal of the star-gazers, their ringing was to announce the exact moment when the laborers should start the work. But before the sages gave the signal, a raven perched on one of the ropes and set the bells ringing. Laborers began their work immediately. It was an unlucky hour. In the first place the raven was taken as a bad omen. Besides, the planet Mars, *Al-Qahir*, was in the ascendant. But it could not be undone. The place, therefore, was named after the hostile planet Al-Qahir (the triumphant) in the hope that the unlucky omen might turn into a successful issue. Thus came the name Al-Qahira (Cairo) to the capital of Egypt.

Secondly, the Fatimids are important because they founded the famous university mosque of Al-Azhar, which has ever since been the world center of Moslem culture. It is today the cultural Mecca of Moslems wherever they are. The number of students in this great university, with all its affiliated institutions, now exceeds thirty thousand. The colleges of the university level belonging to Al-Azhar enroll about five thousand students, of which six hundred are foreigners.

Al-Azhar University, which is now one thousand years old, is not to be confused with the other recently founded universities of modern Egypt. It may be considered as a huge institute for the study of Islamic theology. The Moslem cultural traditions are well preserved in this university, which is the oldest university in the world. The name "Al-Azhar" is again an Arabic word meaning the blooming. The same Fatimid general, Gawhar, who founded and named Al-Qahira (Cairo) in the year 969, was also the founder in 973 of the university mosque of Al-Azhar. The successive rulers of Egypt have at all times favored this institution, partly from academic, partly from political motives. As this university recruited its students chiefly from the villagers, its graduates would go back to the villages to exercise the greatest influence on the people. To a large extent, public opinion in Egypt during the Middle Ages, was formed by the Azhar graduates. This was the reason why Napoleon, as soon as he set foot in Egypt, attempted to bring the Azharites on his side. In fact, to the leaders of Al-Azhar, Egypt owes very much of its recent political awakening.

This great historical university is now run more or less in accordance with modern ways. But it had been characterized during the Moslem period by a certain type of schooling which is still strongly associated with it in the minds of the people. The lecturer, or *sheikh*, would sit on a chair, surrounded by hundreds of students cross-legged on the ground listening or taking notes. Lecturing always meant the analysis of a certain text. The sheikh placed an acknowledged classic before him, explaining each sentence as he went on. Sometimes one of the more advanced students read the text aloud while the lecturer made commentaries wherever necessary. When a student knew by heart, and could explain the book which was studied by the class, the sheikh gave him a testimonial, usually written in the student's copy of the work being studied. By such a testimonial, or diploma, the student was authorized to lecture on that book. But he would never be included in the teaching staff unless time showed that the circle of his students grew wider and wider.

From the days of the Fatimid dynasty (969-1771), many religious and social festivals have been handed down to the modern Egyptians. Egyptians today, for example, observe certain traditions on the tenth of the first month of the lunar calendar. The month is called *Moharram* and the day is called *Ashura*. In some ways it is like Thanksgiving Day in the United States. A rich meal is usually prepared on the Ashura day to show man's gratitude for God's blessings. Originally it was celebrated by the Fatimids because it was the day on which Hussein, the grandson of the Prophet, fell as a martyr. The Fatimids were so called after Fatima, the Prophet's daughter and the mother of the martyr. They believed that the Moslem caliphate should be confined to the Prophet's family. But although no such belief exists in Egypt now, the Ashura day is still celebrated. Some people believe that on that day Adam and Eve first met after their fall. Noah is also supposed to have left his ark on the day of Ashura.

It was during the reign of the Fatimids that the Crusades began. These wars between the Christian and the Moslem worlds were fought between the eleventh and fourteenth centuries. After the Second Crusade, an able young soldier brought the Fatimid rule to an end. He founded a new ruling dynasty in Egypt, and defended the East against the third Crusade. This was Saladin, whose family was known as the Ayoubids.

The Crusades were not merely wars between two churches. They were also a clash between two patterns of culture. At no other time had the East and the West come into such a close contact.

Most eminent among the Moslem figures of the Crusades was Saladin the ruler of Egypt. Saladin's generosity and personal charm gained him popularity even among the Christians. Sir Walter Scott's novel *Talisman* gives a vivid picture of this many-sided hero. From the day he became ruler of Egypt (he ruled from 1171 to 1193) he had pledged himself solemnly to the Holy War. Saladin, the Egyptian Moslem leader in the early part of the war, was at first on the defensive. His decisive victory over the Christian armies made him the undisputed champion of Islam. The citadel in Cairo, built on the Mokattam hills, remains up to the present day as a standing proof of Saladin's military ability.

Saladin's citadel is now one of the chief landmarks of Cairo. The citadel has so often been restored and remodeled that it is difficult to recognize the original work. The founder's inscription, however, may still be read over an old gate. It says that ". . . the building of this splendid Citadel . . . on the terrace which adds use to beauty, and space to strength, for those who seek the shelter of his power,—was ordered by . . . Saladin. . . ." A magnificent mosque was erected in the citadel about a century ago, thus making the site one of the most interesting places in Cairo. From the site of the citadel, one can obtain a breath-taking view of the large yellowish city, with its countless minarets, domes and lofty buildings.

The Ayoubid dynasty, started by Saladin, ruled Egypt for eighty years (1171-1250). Then came the Mameluk period for over two and a half centuries. The term "Mameluk" means a "Slave sultan." It was common among the rulers in those days to govern through members of their personal retinue. It was, therefore, natural that when a feeble sovereign came to power, or when a ruler died suddenly without a successor, the government of the country passed over to the household reti-nue who were in real authority. That was what happened on the unexpected death of the last monarch of the Ayoubid fam-ily in the year 1250. His Mameluks (i.e. slaves) came to power and ran the Empire on their own.

Recruited from the slave-markets of Georgia (between the Black Sea and the Caspian Sea) to serve as the Ayoubid dynasty bodyguard, they soon acquired such authority as to be able to destroy, in 1250, that dynasty and to elect as sultan of Egypt one of their chiefs.

A good number of those Mameluks proved to be able war-riors and efficient administrators. In their days the Mongol barbarians moved from their Asiatic center toward the west, destroying everything on their way. But for the military abil-ity of some Mameluks, the whole Moslem culture in the Middle East might have gone forever.

In the days of the Mameluks, who ruled before the Ottoman invasion of Egypt in 1517, Egypt attained its highest standard in culture during the Middle Ages. The vast majority of the Islamic splendid art monuments, which are still to be seen almost everywhere in Cairo, has been left from the Mameluk days. They built magnificent mosques and great palaces which were masterpieces. They lived in luxury. The tales of the *Arabian Nights* which were composed in Egypt in the Mameluk days, reflected in many ways their luxurious life and economic prosperity. Yet it is a pity that, while the ruling and rich classes lived in such material comfort, the people at large suffered. Irrigation works were neglected, and much of the cultivable land turned into either swamps or wasteland.

Architecture seems to be the divine gift of the Egyptians. In all the stages of their long history, their buildings spoke highly of their talent in this respect. Three cities now stand in Egypt as huge museums telling the story of architecture in this country: Luxor (ancient Thebes) with its vast area of temples and colonnades left by the ancient Egyptians; Alexandria with the remains of the Greco-Roman period; and Cairo with the beautiful mosques, houses and tombs of the early Moslem days.

Compare a temple of ancient Egypt to a mosque of the Middle Ages, and you will be comparing two quite different civilizations. Both buildings were meant for worship in two different religious climates. The former represented splendor, while the latter represented beauty. The ideal of the former was power, while the ideal of the latter was gracefulness and delicacy. It will be observed that when the Moslems built their mosques, they were careful to avoid every resemblance to the pagan buildings. Hence the wide disparity in art between the temples of ancient Amon and the mosques of God-worshiping Moslems.

The most characteristic parts of a mosque are the minaret and the dome. The minaret, from the balconies of which the muezzin calls Moslems to prayer, is generally square at the base, tapering upwards until it ends at the top in a cylindrical shape. Moslem architects showed their greatest skill in building the towering minarets of the mosques. Look at a minaret and you will never fail to notice its strikingly graceful proportions. Inside there is a winding staircase leading to the balconies of the different stories.

Domes are sometimes of considerable height. The summits are often adorned with knobs and crescents. A general view of Cairo is fascinating with its hundreds of minarets and domes towering high in the sky. These splendid mosques, built by unknown architects, are the equivalent, in the Moslem world, of the great cathedrals left in Europe by the Christian Middle Ages.

The interior decorations of a mosque generally consist of panels or flat paintings. The panel decorations are either foliage, geometrical figures or written words. Color does not play an important part in decorating the walls. The ornamental carvings, however, are so skillfully done that they often resemble a network of lace. A striking feature of Moslem art in the Middle Ages is the scarcity of animal pictures, and the absence altogether of human figures.

Perhaps the finest monument of Moslem architecture in Cairo is the Sultan Hassan mosque, built in the years 1356-59. In size, this building reminds us of the ancient Egyptian temples. Its huge gateway, sixty feet high, is important in the history of art, as it has been imitated in the entrances to many other famous mosques all over the Moslem world. Its minaret, two hundred eighty feet high, is the highest in Cairo. The huge proportions of the building, together with the magnificent decorative details, give the spectator an impression of splendor, beauty and majesty.

Architecture, however, was not the only aspect of Moslem culture in Egypt. Names of world-famous scholars can be mentioned in all fields of learning. Among these scholars was Ibn Al-Haytham (known to the writers of the West by the name Al-Hazen), who was born about the year 965 and died in 1038. No less than a hundred works on mathematics, astronomy, philosophy and medicine are ascribed to him. His chief work, however, was on optics. Almost all medieval and Renaissance writers on this subject in Europe depended on his work. Roger Bacon, Leonardo da Vinci and Kepler referred to him. He discovered, in theory, the magnifying lens which was actually made for the first time in Europe several centuries later. While he was imprisoned for some time in a small dark room, he made use of his unlucky situation, by developing the idea of the camera obscura which was the basis of photography. His work was translated into Latin, and was used in the universities of Europe until as late as the seventeenth century.

In the field of pure Islamic studies, such as koranic interpretations and the like, Egypt has produced many a brilliant name. It has also produced a number of historians whose work is highly esteemed by any modern scholar of history. Al-Makrizi (1364-1442) can be taken as a perfect example of a good historian. He wrote a large number of books, ranging from short monographs to a series of huge volumes. There has recently been discovered a bundle of the cards by means of which he recorded and classified his material. These cards prove that he worked on just the same lines as a modern historian.

From among a long list of poets and prose writers, we can content ourselves with one example: the poet Zuheir (died 1258). The Egyptian spirit is accurately reflected in his poetry. In his verses, he gives us a vivid picture of the happy society of early Mameluk times. Among the upper classes there seemed to have been no strict observance of Moslem rules of a moderate way of life. The gay courtiers of the ruling houses indulged in pleasures. The wine cup is as prominent in Zuheir's poems as in Omar Khayyam's. But in the literature of those days, drink was never mentioned without the accompaniment of music and song. This is quite clear in the *Arabian Nights* which were, in part, composed in Egypt in the Middle Ages. In fact, in all forms of art Egypt reached a very high standard in the Mameluk days. Many artists found refuge in Egypt when the barbarian Mongols overran other parts of the Middle East. This artistic contribution was coupled with enormous wealth gained from prosperous commerce with the outside world, to produce luxury that can be seen in the countless monuments in Cairo, left from the Islamic period.

With the Ottoman Turks conquering Egypt in 1517, the country sank into the darkest phase of her Moslem period. Three centuries (1517-1798) of Turkish tyranny and plunder brought the rich and artistic country of Egypt to the pitiful state in which Napoleon found her in the year 1798. The Turks took to their own country most of the artisans of Egypt. With a few exceptions, no longer was Cairo the scene of new masterpieces of architecture. Beautiful decorations disappeared with the skillful decorators.

Never had Egypt been so seriously impoverished. The country at the time was divided into regions for taxation purposes. A government agent was appointed for each region. He was to pay to the administration a certain amount of money. He was then left freehanded to levy from the people whatever other money he could. Farmers and traders were tortured to pay heavy taxes.

The discovery of the sea route to India around Cape Town had, in time, ruined further the economy of Egypt. Before this discovery, the route of commerce between the Far East and Europe was through the Red Sea, then by land from Suez to Alexandria, and finally across the Mediterranean to Venice or Genoa. Both on entering and leaving Egypt, transit taxes were levied. The Portuguese were the first to attempt another route to India. Shortly afterwards Columbus, too, wanted to find a way to India. When it was known that Columbus' voyage ended, not with India, but with a new continent, the Portuguese resumed their attempt. At last Vasco da Gama succeeded in the discovery of the route around Cape Town. The discovery, in the long run, was a final blow to Egypt's prosperity. The consequences were felt at their gravest in the days of the Ottoman rule.

6

EGYPT IN THE ARABIAN NIGHTS

THE *Arabian Nights*, OR THE BOOK OF ONE THOUSAND NIGHTS AND ONE NIGHT—if we stick to the literal translation of the original title—is really one of the most charming collections of folk tales known in literature. It has been translated into almost all the languages of the world. In one abridged form or another, it is read everywhere. Its stories have been frequently used as a basis for entertainment on the stage and in the movies. It certainly appeals to human nature, otherwise it would never be the rich source of literary treasure that it has proved to be.

Nobody knows who were the original storytellers of this wonderful collection of tales. Many scholars have made it the subject of long and serious study. Certain facts are now agreed upon. In the first place, the book was not all written at one and the same age or in one and the same country. Like a truly living being, it grew in the course of time. Parts from here were piled on parts from there until it took its final form. But it was in Egypt of the Middle Ages that the whole material was retold and remodeled to achieve a unity of spirit and atmosphere.

The tales of the *Arabian Nights* may generally be divided

into three groups. First, there is the Indo-Persian group of tales, the origin of which was either India or Persia. These were translated into the Arabic language during the eighth century, and can be easily picked out by the names of people or the names of places. Second, there is the Baghdad group which pictures the golden days of wealth and prosperity in the Moslem capital, the city of Baghdad, during the tenth and eleventh centuries. It will be observed, and this is a very important point, that the picture is literary but not literal. An imaginary description of an age is not a true and historical description of that age, even though it depicts its spirit correctly. Was there ever a knight who behaved in the manner of Don Quixote? Yet Don Quixote is a marvelous picture of knighthood in the Middle Ages. And this is the case with the descriptions in the tales of the *Arabian Nights*. Harun-al-Rashid's court in Baghdad is luxuriously described from the point of view of a public storyteller who had never seen the caliph's palace. It is the picture a poor man would form for himself about the life of the rich.

The third group of tales originated in Egypt during the fourteenth and fifteenth centuries. But this was not the only role played by the Egyptian storytellers in the formation of the book. As has already been said, the older parts, the Indian, Persian and Baghdadian parts, were retold in the public entertainment places in Egypt, and were radically modified to fit in with the taste of the Egyptian audience. Hence, it may well be assumed that the whole collection of the *Arabian Nights* reflects the social life of Egypt in the Middle Ages, either directly or indirectly. Even when the foreign outline was retained, thousands of details were added by the Egyptian storyteller to make the story appealing to the Egyptian listener. The book took its final shape in Egypt at about the end of the fifteenth century.

The tales of the *Arabian Nights*, however, do not give us a comprehensive picture of Egypt in those days. They have almost exclusively concentrated on city life rather than the life in the country. The peasants are not mentioned. In a country where the chief occupation of the people was, and still is, agriculture, this is very strange. Traders and artisans in the city were the main body of people about whom the tales were told. Nevertheless, the teller would seize any opportunity in the course of his tale to divert from his main line and tell us something about other lands and other people. A very common technique was to make the merchant or the craftsman, about whom the story was told, leave the country on a business tour. The city of Basra, on the Persian Gulf, was frequently chosen as the destination of the traveling merchant. There he would not only carry out business, but would meet people, especially important people, fall in love and get married, or fall in a trap plotted by conspirators. While telling us about his adventures in the foreign land and among the foreign people, he also tells us many strange imaginary things: magic carpets, enchanted places, miracles achieved by fairies and jinn, and the like.

To stimulate the imagination of his audience, the teller often chose a distant place, or a remote time in the past for his scene. This trick also gave him liberty to tell whatever strange things he chose. China was one of the faraway countries often chosen. The adventurers would also go to mysterious caves, or would be moved on magic carpets to unknown places. To distance in space, the teller added remoteness in time. Seldom did he tell about "yesterday" or "last year." He always told about things that he assumed to have taken place in the remote past.

The sympathy of the teller was always with the poor craftsman against the man of authority or the man of enormous wealth. Whenever a comparison is drawn the storyteller always points out that a modest living honestly earned is of a higher value than a wicked though financially successful way of life. It is interesting to notice how the teller always finds a way of escape for the poor but honest people. Many a time a man of virtue falls into difficulties then all of a sudden, he comes across hidden treasure, or even meets a miraculous figure who helps him out.

Licentious as the book may seem, it is always, in the end, a defense of virtue. A man or a woman may go morally astray, but never has immorality been allowed to go without penalty. Love between the two sexes, of course, looms large in the *Arabian Nights*. But a searching look will clearly show that moral standards are lurking behind the apparently loose behavior.

What is of a special interest to us here is the fact that many parts of the *Arabian Nights* give us a true picture of the Egyptian city life in the Middle Ages. Whenever you come across a tale about a merchant's adventures or a craftsman's business, or a tale about smart people, or a tale about the use of magic in employing the supernatural creatures for the service of human beings, and above all, wherever you come across a tale of wit and humor, then it is more likely that it is a tale of the Egyptian group. Perhaps nothing among historical writings can give us a more vivid and more detailed picture of the Egyptian way of life in those days. National feasts are well described. What people did on such occasions is to a large extent what people still do. Wedding ceremonies, rejoicing at the birth of a baby, the celebration of the seventh day after the baby's birth, the attempt to guard babies against the evil eyes of envy, these are among many aspects of social life accurately pictured. Human relations—how the members of a family were related to one another, how much parents loved their children, how much authority a father had over his family, what the relation was like between governor and governed, and thousands of other similar things—are portrayed in the *Arabian Nights*. Perhaps best pictured are the different ways of spending leisure, the various ways of entertainment and having a good time, the musical instruments used, and the kinds of songs that were hummed on different occasions.

The *Arabian Nights* is not the only folklore of Egypt. There is another group of tales which is much closer to the people's minds and hearts. They are mainly tales of love and chivalry. Even today this latter group of tales is often told in coffee-shops, especially on certain occasions. They strongly appeal to the masses, both in the town and the countryside.

On such occasions, particularly on the evenings of public festivals, a professional teller is hired by the keeper of a coffee-shop. He sits on a high seat at one side of the shop. His listeners, who are the customers of the café, arrange themselves comfortably. While listening, they enjoy their coffee or tea or whatever their drink may be. They usually get so engrossed in the story that they identify themselves with the characters. The recitation is always partly dramatized and accompanied by the music of some sort of a lyre. Hence, the narrator is known by the audience as "the poet."

7

A CENTURY OF AWAKENING

With the french campaign led by napoleon in the year 1798, Egypt started a new era in her history. Her middle ages came to an end and a modern period began. During the Turkish rule (1517-1798) the country gradually sank into a sorrowful state of affairs. The peasants were pillaged. Corruption prevailed. Intrigues never ceased. A viceroy ruled the country for the sultan of Turkey. But, the sultan himself had preserved the Mameluks (see Chapter 5) as a check on the viceroy who governed in his name. Apparently, everything was done according to the viceroy's orders. In reality, the viceroy was helpless. The real authority was in the Mameluks' hands. And so long as the tribute was regularly paid, the sultan of Constantinople had no cause for interference.

Such a state of affairs could not but attract the eyes of the outside world and suggested to Napoleon the idea of conquering Egypt. Among his chief aims in this was to stand in Britain's way to India. Napoleon planned to defeat the English but he put in their mind the idea of taking Egypt for themselves. Britain's interest was aroused by the news of the French Expedition leaving Toulon for an unknown destination. The British fleet under Nelson immediately went in search of the French ships. Nelson rightly guessed that Egypt might be Napoleon's aim. Shortly after the landing of the French at Alexandria, and while Napoleon was busy fighting the battle of the Pyramids with the Mameluks of Egypt (July 1798), Nelson utterly destroyed the French ships at Abukir near Alexandria. Thus blockaded, Napoleon felt the gravity of his situation. He soon returned to France, leaving his forces behind under Kleber's command. In 1801, the French were compelled by a British army to evacuate Egypt.

The French military expedition was accompanied by a hundred scholars in various fields: mechanics, engineers, architects, hydrologists, authors, archaeologists. They brought with them an Arabic printing press. The French leader envisaged the written word as more powerful than armament and gunpowder. The Arabic printing press thus introduced, was the first to be used in Egypt. It was a real starting point of a new phase in Egypt's culture. The French savants did research in their different branches, and wrote such a detailed description of Egypt that their combined work still remains a valuable source of knowledge. It has been truly said that considering the effect, the French Expedition was rather academic than military. Chief among the points raised by the French scholars was the problem of joining the Red Sea to the Mediterranean with a canal. But after calculations, it was wrongly thought that the water level in the Red Sea was thirty-three feet higher than the water level in the Mediterranean. The project was thus given up for the time being.

Back went Egypt to the Turkish Sultan. Mohammed Ali, an ambitious Albanian soldier in the Turkish army, gradually rose to power. In 1805 he was appointed by the sultan, as viceroy of Egypt. The Egyptians themselves showed signs of satisfaction with such a choice. But the Mameluks were still an impending danger. As the result of a successful plot, a large number of them were gathered inside the citadel and assassinated. The way was now clear before Mohammed Ali.

In a few years' time, the new ruler had built up a strong army. It was obvious to him from the first that he had to rely on Egyptian recruits for his army. But this had to be achieved gradually. The Egyptians had been deprived of military activities throughout the long Turkish rule. Before Mohammed Ali, the Egyptian farmers had been regarded as laborers who should industriously and patiently raise money and crops for the tax-collectors. Military service had been confined to the Mameluks. The *fellahin*, Egyptian farmers, were said to lack the military qualities of discipline and courage. To provide his army with well-equipped Egyptian officers, Mohammed Ali had just to establish an educational system. A new army and a new educational system were, therefore, born together. Both were planned on Western lines. Thus began the trends in modern Egypt. With his newly formed army, Mohammed Ali fought the Wahhabites in Arabia and captured Mecca and Medina. In the year 1823 the Sudan was conquered and the city of Khartoum was founded. Now the whole valley of the Nile was in his hand.

Expansionist wars continued. Syria was taken in 1832. Constantinople itself was about to fall. But here European powers intervened. Britain's future Prime Minister Palmerston wrote at the time that "Mohamed Aly will just be chucked in the Nile. It would certainly be a good thing if he could be got rid of altogether, yet that is improbable for he will give in long before matters come to such a point. We do not want to oust him from Egypt if he is content to spend the rest of his days there as a faithful servant."

Mohammed Ali was forced to yield. He had to quit Syria and Arabia. In return, he was given in 1841, the hereditary sovereignty of Egypt. An annual tribute was to be paid by him to the Sultan of Turkey. Mohammed Ali died in the year 1849, leaving the country to his heirs.

During the reign of Mohammed Ali, the cotton plant was introduced into Egypt, it was soon to become the principal product of the country. Since cotton grows in summer when the Nile River is too low to feed the canals running through the fields, a dam was planned to be built at the head of the delta. It was meant to keep the water of the Nile at a level that would make irrigation possible. Although begun in the days of Mohammed Ali, the dam was not completed and ready for use until 1883. In order to use Alexandria's harbor for exporting cotton, a canal was dug to connect the seaport with the Nile. This canal, in effect, brought Alexandria back to its long neglected importance. By the same canal a vast area of cultivatable land was irrigated.

In spite of the fact that Mohammed Ali established a sound basis for a new Egypt, yet he was a real despot with no respect for the rights of the individual. Men were forced into digging canals, into growing cotton, into working in factories, into serving in the army and whatever else the ruler wanted them to do.

Fifteen years after Mohammed Ali's death, the Suez Canal question was raised again. Ferdinand de Lesseps secured in 1854 the approval of Sa'id, the khedive of Egypt, for a canal to be constructed to join the Red Sea to the Mediterranean. In fact this was only a new chapter in a long story.

As early as the year 1380 B.C. Siti I, Egypt's Pharaoh at the time, had the two seas connected, for the first time, by a canal joining the Red Sea to the Nile. A ship might thereby enter from the Red Sea into the canal, and then sail down the River Nile to the Mediterranean. In course of time the canal fell into disuse. Later, in the year 609 B.C. another ruler, Necho, made a second attempt. But before completing his project an oracle dissuaded him from going on. Such a canal, the oracle advised, would serve the enemy rather than Egypt herself. King Darius in 520 B.C. completed the unfinished canal. But again it was neglected and became unfit for navigation until the Arab conquest of Egypt. In the year A.D. 640 Amr Ibn el-Aas reviewed the project. His purpose was to create a quick and easy way of transporting wheat from Egypt to the drought-stricken Arabia. Finally, in 770 the caliph at Baghdad, by way of punishing a rebellious governor in Arabia, gave orders that the food-carrying canal should be destroyed.

With the accession of Sa'id in 1854 the project was brought up for consideration. The khedive signed a concession for a Frenchman De Lesseps, but this was subject to the approval of the Turkish sultan which De Lesseps went to Constantinople to obtain. But the British representative convinced the sultan that the projected canal would lead to the severance of Egypt from Turkey and to the interposition of a French colony on the canal. British statesmen realized that just as the Indian Empire was created by merchants, the same kind of empire might be created in Egypt by the French. Besides, it was feared that the project, when completed, might jeopardize Britain's sea supremacy. The sultan's permission, however, was at last secured.

A considerable time elapsed before the necessary capital was raised. The cost of constructing the canal was more than half paid by Egypt. The work of digging was actually begun in 1859. It was stipulated that four-fifths of the workmen should be Egyptians. This was interpreted by the company to mean that the government had to provide and maintain 25,000 workmen who were to be replaced by others every three months. The conscript labor was so hard that over 120,000 workers lost their lives in the process, with no indemnities to their families. Again the supply of fresh water presented a difficulty. A fresh water canal was therefore constructed from near Cairo to the Suez zone. The company was given the right to charge the farmers for using its water. It was agreed that the profit accrued from the Suez Canal should be divided as follows: (after paying 5 per cent interest on the shareholders' capital and the reserve fund) 15 per cent to the Egyptian Government, 10 per cent to the founders of the company, and 75 per cent to the shareholders and management. The duration of the contract with the company was limited to ninety-nine years. By the end of this period in 1968, the Egyptian Government would have had possession of the company's property and taken over the management of the canal.

The Suez Canal was officially opened by Ismail, the khedive of Egypt, in the year 1869. The extravagant festivities that took place on the occasion cost Egypt about twelve million dollars. To entertain his distinguished guests from Europe, the khedive had *Aida*, specially composed by Verdi, played in the specially built opera house in Cairo.

Ismail (1863-1879) having exhausted the finances of the country, had to resort to foreign loans. The road was thus paved for foreign powers to interfere with Egypt's affairs. The moment of crisis came in 1875. Ismail was unable to pay the interest on his loans, or, rather, unable to raise new loans to pay the interest on the old. He, therefore, sold Egypt's shares in the canal (amounting to nearly half the total number of shares) to Britain for 4 million pounds. When, three years later, this proved to be still inadequate to pay his further debts, he allowed England and France to establish financial control over Egypt. Ismail's debts now reached 68 million pounds. A British Minister of Finance and a French Minister of Public Works were appointed members in the Egyptian Cabinet, and were given an absolute veto. And finally the story came to its logical end when Ismail was told by a British representative that: "The French and English Governments are agreed to advise your Highness officially to abdicate and to leave Egypt."

Tewfik succeeded his dethroned father. He was a mere puppet in the hands of the foreign controllers who were the actual rulers of Egypt. The real interests of the Egyptians were disregarded, either for the sake of the foreign financiers or for that of the Turkish element inside the country. A movement of resentment started with the Egyptian officers in the army. Ahmed Arabi was the leader. To begin with he presented a protest to the khedive about the maltreatment of the Egyptian officers as compared with the non-Egyptians in the army. Instead of replying to the protest, the khedive planned Arabi's arrest. But Arabi's compatriots in the army released him by force. On September 9, 1881, Arabi and his men filled the square in front of the khedive's palace and presented their national demands. In a dramatic scene, the khedive arrived accompanied by the British consul. Arabi approached them on horseback. The khedive ordered him to dismount. He did so, came forward on foot and saluted. Asked what all that meant, Arabi answered: "We are no longer slaves, we shall not be handed from one master to another." And then he demanded that certain reforms be introduced.

The khedive temporarily yielded to the demands of the army, among which was the convocation of a parliament. But the Arabi movement had many enemies, and could hardly be expected to function without conflict. The sultan of Turkey, the nominal sovereign of the country, felt his authority was threatened. The local Turks in Egypt feared they might lose their supremacy. The khedive foresaw that his dynasty was in danger. The French and the British found the whole situation an opportunity not to be missed for increasing their influence. Both of them wanted to support the khedive, but each of them tried to outwit the other in the game.

Egyptian public opinion was now behind the national movement led by Arabi. The situation became so tense that each party made itself ready for serious conflict. Arabi expected a naval attack on Alexandria by the British and French. The harbor of Alexandria was, therefore, fortified. Guns were mounted at the entrance of the harbor. The British Government ordered their admiral in the Mediterranean to open fire on Arabi's defenses and destroy them. This intervention was too much even for Britain's ally, the French, who officially declared that France would not associate herself with such an overt act of hostility against Egypt.

Britain seized the opportunity to act alone. On July 11,

1882, Alexandria was bombarded by the British fleet. Expecting that the British forces would land in Alexandria, Arabi stood near by prepared for battle. He was assured by De Lesseps that the British would not use the neutral Suez Canal for military purposes. Nevertheless, it was from the Suez Canal that the British took Arabi by surprise. Arabi hurried from his position near Alexandria to meet them somewhere near Suez. But he lost the battle of Tel-el-Kebir. And thus began the British occupation of Egypt.

Almost simultaneously with the British occupation of Egypt, there arose in the Egyptian Sudan a revolution led by al-Mahdi. In 1885 Khartoum fell in the hands of the rebels, and the Egyptian force in the Sudan was instructed to evacuate, thereby bringing the all-Egyptian rule of the Sudan to an end. But in 1898 the Sudan was placed theoretically under an Anglo-Egyptian administration. In reality, the administration of the Sudan was entirely in the hands of the British. It was in 1954 that the Sudan finally secured its independence.

During their occupation of Egypt, the British economic policy laid the stress on agriculture and stifled industry. Egypt was looked upon as a large cotton-producing farm. The irrigation system was therefore given much care. Dams were built and canals were dug throughout the country. Most important of all the irrigation schemes was the Aswan Dam constructed at the farthest end of the country to the south.

A mixture of despair at the present and hope for the future caused an active intellectual movement to arise in Egypt in the 1880's and after. Al-Afghani was its prime mover. His purpose was to bring about a rebirth of the Moslem world. Distinguished among his followers was Mohammed Abdu. He developed his master's purpose until it became a kind of reformation program. Abdu's influence spread throughout the whole Islamic world. Students and admirers formed what was known as Abdu's party. Their main problem was how to adapt the Islamic faith to the sudden impact of the new conditions. Mohammed Abdu and his followers believed that for a Moslem country to get rid of its foreign rule, it had to begin with an intellectual reform. Religious superstition had to be removed from people's minds as a necessary step towards enlightenment.

With the British occupying the country, and the intellectual leaders stirring the people to a lively awakening, the curtain of the nineteenth century fell.

8

INDEPENDENT EGYPT

WHEN BRITAIN OCCUPIED EGYPT IN 1882, SHE MADE IT CLEAR that the occupation was only temporary. Some nationalists hoped that even if the British did not withdraw, France, at any rate, would not keep silent. But in 1904 both countries, Brittain and France, agreed that the former should be given free hand in Egypt, while the latter should be left undisturbed in North West Africa.

A nationalist party, led by young Mustafa Kamil, was soon to appear in 1907 to demand the British withdrawal. "A new spirit," wrote the young leader, "has been born within us. More than ever before we now realise that nations cannot rise without themselves struggling for their own cause. We cannot win independence by help from others. We have to work for it ourselves. Like an individual, a nation must be strong and well-equipped to defend its honor, life and property. Those who count on others to secure independence are deluded." Contrary to Mohammed Abdu who thought that intellectual reform was the means to political independence, Mustafa Kamil believed that no reform would be of any avail as long as foreign troops occupied the country.

In 1914 World War I broke out. Britain declared that Egypt was now her protectorate. The nationalist movement remained temporarily silent. But just on the morrow of Armistice Day, the Egyptians resumed their political struggle. On November 13, 1918, a group of national leaders, headed by Saad Zaghlul, demanded from the British High Commissioner in Cairo that Egypt should be allowed to send her representatives to the Paris Peace Conference, where she might claim her right to complete independence. The demand was rejected. The nationalist spirit immediately flared up, and revolution broke out.

Negotiations for a settlement began between Britain and Egypt. On February 28, 1922, Egypt was declared an independent country, but with certain reservations. Another treaty, which gave more rights to Egypt, was concluded between the two countries in 1936. According to this latter agreement, Britain was given a free hand in the Suez Canal Zone.

In 1945, after World War II Egypt strongly urged that the 1936 treaty should be revised. The British declined to meet Egypt's desire and a state of political unrest prevailed.

Israel was created in 1948. Public opinion within the Arab states forced Egypt to protest. The Egyptian army, inadequately equipped, was sent into battle by a king and government not so much interested in the cause as in how to win money and popularity. They made money out of bargain-basement arms. They won popularity by playing the heroes in a cause based on patriotic appeal. "But though cut off," remarks an English writer, "though ill-equipped, though neglected by gluttonous politicians in Cairo, these Egyptian soldiers fought with a heroism which has not received its due in western accounts." At Falouga a garrison held out under total siege for four months. A twenty-nine-year-old officer was to write afterwards: "Falouga was then under siege, and the enemy had concentrated their guns and aircraft heavily on it. Often I said to myself: 'Here we are in these underground holes, besieged. We have been cheated into a war for which we were unprepared, and our destinies have been the plaything of passions, plots, and greed. Here we lie under fire unarmed.' As I reached that stage in my thoughts, my feelings would suddenly leap across the battlefront, across frontiers, to Egypt. I found myself saying, 'There is our country, a far, far bigger Falouga. What is happening in Falouga is only what is happening in Egypt, in miniature. She too has been besieged by difficulties, as well as ravaged by an enemy. She too has been cheated and pushed into a fight for which she was not prepared. Greed, intrigue and passion have used her as a plaything, too, and have placed her under fire, without arms.'" The same officer felt, while besieged at Falouga, that a unity of the Arab world was the only way out for the Middle East countries from their sufferings. "I came back from Palestine," Gamal Abdel-el-Nasser, now the President of United Arab Republic, was to write, "with the Arab world as one complete whole in my mind."

Indignation and bitterness filled the hearts and souls of all the Egyptians, except King Farouk and his clique. In January, 1952, the people in Cairo expressed their discontent in a manner both regrettable and significant. They burned down a good number of important buildings in their own city. This indicated that the country was on the brink of complete ruin or that only a miracle would save her from the abyss. The miracle did happen a few months later.

On July 23, 1952, a group of young officers in the army,

who had been plotting since the disaster of the Palestine war in 1948, brought their plan into action. Their success was complete and decisive. Early in the morning of that day, an announcement stated that Cairo was now in the hands of a Revolutionary Command. Three days later King Farouk was forced to leave the country. With his departure came the end of Mohammed Ali's dynasty. Shortly afterwards, Egypt was proclaimed a republic.

But although the old regime had given way to a new era, yet the Suez Canal Zone was still occupied by British troops. This last remnant of foreign control had to be removed, if Egypt was to attain full independence both from within and from without. In 1954, an agreement was signed by Egypt and Britain to the effect that Egypt would regain her national territory, while the British would have the right to reoccupy the Suez base under certain conditions. But this agreement was nullified when Egypt was attacked in 1956 by Britain, together with France and Israel, as a result of the nationalization of the Suez Canal Company. And Egypt is now for the first time, after so many centuries of foreign rule, a fully independent country.

Egypt's success has aroused a long-cherished hope in the hearts of the people of the other Arab states—the hope for unity among the Arabs. Although an Arab League had been existent since 1945 to bring the various Arab states into the desired unity, yet the unity expressed therein was more formal than real. The first serious step towards a real unity was taken in February, 1958, by Egypt and Syria. Since then, Egypt has taken the name United Arab Republic.

9

CAIRO AND ALEXANDRIA

MARCHING ALONG THE MEDITERRANEAN COAST OF EGYPT, ALEX-
ander the Great passed by the island of Pharos, a few miles to
the west of the Nile Delta. It was the same Pharos which was
mentioned in Homer's *Odyssey*. Ulysses referred to it as his
beloved isle.

Opposite Pharos on the mainland was a small fishing village.
Alexander felt that an ideal harbor could be created by joining
the island of Pharos with the village on the shore. It would
serve as a seaport for his relations with the rest of the world.
The idea was carried out. Thus began Alexandria, Egypt's second largest city.

Landing in Alexandria, one cannot help recalling the great
panorama of history that the city has witnessed. One can go
back in one's imagination to the famous museum when it was
the center of world culture, the meeting place of distinguished
scholars. Marcus Aurelius (161-180) attended the lectures
here. Alexandria was the residence of such great thinkers as
Philo, Plotinus and Euclid. Connected with the museum was
the library well-known in history. In the days of Caesar the
library contained about 900,000 scrolls. But that priceless
treasure was all lost when the building was burned in Caesar's
time.

In addition to being a center of learning, Alexandria was one of the earliest cities to adopt Christianity; there the Gospel was preached to the Alexandrians by St. Mark.

Modern Alexandria is built on the site of the ancient city and therefore little of the Greco-Roman period remains. Many ancient spots, however, can be identified. It is thrilling to realize while walking along Liberty Street and Nabi Daniel Street, that these were two of the most important thoroughfares in Alexandria twenty centuries ago. Cleopatra must have passed here. Perhaps Mark Antony or Caesar walked on this same ground and under this same sky.

The only ancient monument which still remains is Pompey's Pillar. It is mistakenly given this name as it had nothing to do with Pompey. The pillar was erected to carry the statue of Diocletian (A.D. 302). It was also meant to serve as a landmark for sailors.

The old lighthouse of Alexandria, built in 280 B.C. on the island of Pharos, and which was counted as one of the seven wonders of the world, exists no more. It was destroyed by an earthquake in A.D. 1375. In its place stands a new lighthouse which can be seen from a distance of nineteen miles out in the sea.

Yet a great deal of the story of ancient Alexandria can be learned by a visit to the Greco-Roman Museum in the city. While there, it is interesting to compare the art of the period (from the third century B.C. to the third century A.D.) with the art of the earlier period. Both were Egyptian art, but the one differed widely from the other. Contrast the white marble Greco-Roman statues with the dark granite statues of older Egypt. They represent two phases of civilization. In their frailty and ease the Greco-Roman statues look human, while in their sobriety and splendor, the pharaonic statues express the majesty of the superhuman.

Alexandria has two harbors. Unlike ancient times, it is the west harbor which is used today for big ships. It is protected by a breakwater about two miles long. Near the west harbor, the canal, which connects the city with the Nile, enters the sea. This canal is the source of drinking water for Alexandria, as well as one of the main highways joining the city with the rest of the country.

The population of Alexandria today exceeds one million. Large European communities live here. The atmosphere of the city is, therefore, nearest to that of a European seaport.

Along the shore, there extends an ever-growing chain of beaches linked together by a promenade several miles long. In the summer, tens of thousands of holiday-makers bathe and bask on the beautiful sands.

Yachting and fishing are common sports in Alexandria. On the very spot where Cleopatra had her palace and temple twenty centuries ago, there is now an excellent club for fishing and sailing.

A short distance to the east of Alexandria lies the fishing village of Abukir where the naval battle between Napoleon and Nelson took place in 1798.

The age-old cultural spirit of this great city is today carried on in its university. Its enrollment is nineteen thousand students (1958). Girls account for about ten per cent of this number. There are schools for all the branches of learning, with a special stress on the studies related to the sea.

With its long and glorious history, its delightful climate all year round, its lighthearted, lively and witty people, its fascinating beaches, its busy markets and harbors, its numerous clubs and casinos, its cosmopolitan atmosphere, Alexandria is really one of the most charming cities in the world.

About one hundred years ago, the first train left Alexandria for Cairo. The railway between the two cities was one of the first ever built. It was constructed by Robert Stephenson, son of George Stephenson, the inventor of the locomotive

After a three-hour train trip from Alexandria, we arrive at Egypt's capital, one of the biggest, oldest and most interesting of cities. Present-day Cairo is inhabited by two and a half million people. It is spread over an area four times as great as Paris, and is still rapidly growing. It is a strange and colorful mixture of the old and new, the past and present, the East and West.

In Cairo's Geographical Society, there is a chart illustrating how the city, like an embryo gradually taking shape, has developed in the last thousand years from the simple quarters that it was, to the expanding metropolis that it is today. In the early stages of its development, Cairo spread away from the Nile toward the northeast, creeping closer and closer to the Mokattam hills. During the last century, the direction of growth turned toward the river, extended toward the west. It is understandable then that the medieval atmosphere prevails in the eastern side, while the modern spirit predominates in the western.

Coming out of the railway station, one finds oneself in a large square, heavy with traffic of all kinds: automobiles, trucks, buses, streetcars and horse-driven carts. But most outstanding amidst the tumult of the place is the towering statue of Ramses. Comparable in size to the Statue of Liberty at the entrance of New York, the awesome Pharaoh stands high at the door of Egypt's capital to remind the visitor of a glorious past revived in a hopeful present.

This may suggest to the visitor that he should begin his tour with a tribute to the ancient builders of human civilization. After a quick visit to the Sphinx and Pyramids of Giza, ten miles from the center of the city, he may decide to spend some hours in the Museum of the Egyptian Antiquities.

If our reader has already visited the New York Metropolitan Museum of Art, he must have wondered at the ten-room section showing the rich collection of the Egyptian relics. No museum in the world worthy of its name, is without a considerable amount of the Egyptian monuments. But all these vast collections that fill the world museums are only a small part of the immensely rich museum in Cairo.

Let us just have a look at only a few pieces. Here is the statue of Kephren, the builder of the second pyramid. It is said to be the masterpiece of all Egyptian sculpture. To appreciate it best, one should look at it from its side. For the sculptor carved the profiles first on the block of stone, and left the face to be formed by the meeting of the two profiles.

Here is another statue beautifully carved in wood. It is the image of a stout man with a good-natured smile on his lips and a friendly look in his eyes. He has a commanding air emphasized by a cane in his hand. As soon as the diggers unearthed the statue, they were struck by the resemblance it bore to the mayor of their village. They gave him the nickname of "Sheikh el-Balad" (i.e. the village mayor), by which name it is now known.

While still on the ground floor of the museum, we must have a look at the statue of the "Scribe." It is a squatting figure, in a writing position, with attentive eyes and listening ears. The paper is in his lap, and the "scribe" is ready to write down his master's words.

But let us hurry to take a glimpse at the wonder of all wonders: The Tutankhamen treasure. Entering his gallery, we pass between two rows of lifesize human figures made of ebony. Skirts of gold cover their loins. Sandals of gold are on their feet. Headdresses of gold crown their foreheads. Each man holds a staff with a golden ball at one end. These are the guards of King Tutankhamen. They are all on the alert, arranged in the way they were found at the threshold of the king's tomb.

Also on guard is a lifesize hound of ebony, with a gold collar round his neck. Wherever you look in Tutankhamen's halls, your eyes fall on a masterpiece of art. Chariots of gold, chairs of gold, chests, divans and beds, all made of gold. Nowhere else in the world can so much gold in so much art be seen gathered in one place.

Where shall we go next after our hasty visit to the museum? By way of contrast, let us go to the colorful eastern side of Cairo. Here much of the atmosphere of the Middle Ages is retained.

As was the custom in older days, shops of the same kind, with their workshops, are gathered together in the same quarter. The quarter is often named after the goods made or sold in it. There is the bazaar of goldsmiths, the bazaar of coppersmiths, and so on.

The Mousky, with its part which is called Khan el Khalili are the famous bazaars of Cairo. Khan el Khalili goes back in history over five hundred years. At the beginning of the fifteenth century, plans of reconstruction in Cairo were carried out. One of those plans brought together all trades in one quarter. The architect of that new quarter was a man called Girgis el Khalil. Thus the name Khan el Khalili arose.

The streets of the bazaars are but narrow lanes, often covered over with big squares of material to shade them. On both sides of each lane are small shops usually overflowing with a large variety of articles. Artisans work right in their shops, so you can watch their craftsmanship in action. It is interesting to observe skillful hands carving or polishing this or that article, twisting and turning fine silver or gold wires into broaches and bracelets. You can watch the weavers at work interlacing threads of different textures into a variety of fabrics, from ordinary cotton or woollen materials to the finest brocades. Trays, small tables, boxes and other such things, can be seen being inlaid with ebony, ivory or mother of pearl. The medieval atmosphere of the Orient, in this part of Cairo, is emphasized by the odor of spices and perfumes met with everywhere in those bazaars.

Leaving the Mousky and Khan el Khalili bazaars, it is appropriate to make our next visit to some of the famous mosques in Cairo. A large number of these was built in the Middle Ages. In Cairo alone, there are hundreds of mosques interesting both from the historical and artistic points of view. Cairo is often described as the city of four hundred minarets. If Rome is the city of countless churches, Cairo is the city of countless mosques. They all point skywards with charming finger-like minarets.

We shall visit just one mosque, the mosque of Ibn Touloun. It is in the eastern part of the city, near Saladin's citadel. It is one of the oldest mosques in Cairo, built in A.D. 877. We are told that Ibn Touloun, the ruler who had the mosque built in his reign, asked his architects to build him such a monument as would remain forever. It should be, so he demanded, both flood-resistive and fireproof.

One strange aspect of the mosque is its system of arches. They rest on pillars in a cloister-like manner. This particular style of arch was built for the first time in Egypt, and perhaps for the first time in the history of world architecture. It was the origin of the pointed Gothic arch which appeared in France only after the European warriors of the First Crusade had returned home from Egypt and other parts of the Middle East.

Another interesting peculiarity of this mosque is the style of its minaret. Its outer flight of steps gives it the appearance of a spiral. It is said that Ibn Touloun, dissatisfied with the plans of his architect, nervously rolled the plan sheet around his finger. The rolled sheet of paper formed a shape that could be used in building a spiral tower. Suddenly noticing that form, he pointed out to his architect that that was the model of the minaret he wanted. Thus a fine piece of architecture was the offspring of a casual act.

There is a legend about Ibn Touloun's mosque. It is believed, mistakenly of course, that the mosque lies exactly on the spot where Abraham sacrificed the ram instead of his son. Therefore the hilly spot on which the mosque stands, even today is called the "Citadel of the Ram" (the Arabic word for ram is *kabsh*).

Just next door to the mosque of Ibn Touloun is a marvelous piece of art and history and legend, all gathered together in the so-called "House of the Cretans." It is a sixteenth century house recently restored and furnished to re-create all the glamour and all the splendor of a rich family in medieval Cairo.

In the courtyard there is a fountain sprinkling water over stone tortoises. Green plants hang down from earthenware jars. In a corner there is the top of a well. In the floor above, there are a large number of rooms strangely arranged. Every inch of the place presents a wonder of art—carved screens, copperware and brassware, carpets of beautiful designs and divans covered with silk material. The ceilings are painted and decorated. In the alcoves and closets vases and other pieces of art are attractively arranged.

Curious legends are told about the place. Noah's Ark is said to have been stranded here. From the deep well in the house sprang the last waters of the Flood. The following is a charming story related in this connection.

Once, there was a widow of a prince who lived with her only daughter in the House of the Cretans. Zeinab—for that was the name of this young girl—was as beautiful as the moon and as sweet as jasmin. In a neighboring house, lower down the hill, lived Yassine, a handsome young man of a fine family—the only son, also, of a widow. To the disappointment of his mother, he refused to marry and thereby carry on the family name. In vain did his mother sing the praises of this or that young girl endowed with both charm and wealth.

"It is I alone who shall choose my wife," replied Yassine.

"In that case," replied his exasperated mother one day, "you will lose all the young and beautiful girls in the harems, and will end by marrying a divorced woman or a widow. As for me, I shall not tell you a thing more about them—not even about Zeinab, of the House of the Cretans, whom I have just seen."

The curiosity of the young man was suddenly aroused. Who was this Zeinab? What did she look like? Was she slender? With his mind filled with questions, Yassine no longer knew any peace. Zeinab's eyes—were they black and almond-shaped? Her cheeks like pomegranates? Finally, at the end of a week, he was in love with a figure of his imagination and spent the whole day at the window, gazing at the House of the Cretans.

One day as Zeinab looked at the neighboring houses from behind a window, she caught sight of the young man and, staring at him, found herself in love with him. How handsome he was! But how pale!

"He must be in love," Zeinab said to herself. "If only it were I that he loved," she thought, suddenly becoming jealous.

Despite this, she left her observation post, walked slowly through the rooms, and then went down into the courtyard where, at last, she looked down into the water of the well to see if she were beautiful enough to please the young man.

But now, reflecting the pure young face, the water—calm since the Flood—became troubled, and then began to rise, as in the time of Noah. It reached the top, overflowed, spread out and came toward the terrified young girl, who fled from it so quickly that she lost the veil with which she covered her head. She came running down the hill, calling for help, and having at her heels a flood of water the like of which had never been seen before.

From his window Yassine had seen this remarkable occurrence and, rousing his mother, ran down the stairs. He arrived

in time upon the threshold to pull Zeinab into safety and, as
he closed the heavy door behind her, the two clung to each
other in a desperate and passionate embrace.

The flood followed the slope of the road, and finally poured
into the Calif Canal by a little lane, which carries until this
day the name of Sharia el-Bir, the Street of the Well.

Like all such simple and charming tales, this one ends, naturally, with a marriage.

Indeed, to stay in this colorful part of Cairo, the eastern side
with remains of the medieval atmosphere, reliving the past in
your imagination, is to live in a world of dreams.

But a few minutes' walk towards the western side of the city,
will bring you back to the world of today. Cairo stands with
one foot in the past, the other in the atomic age. A new city
of giant buildings has arisen along the banks of the Nile.

Cairo, the city of the Sphinx and Pyramids, of the mosques
and minarets, is rapidly becoming a city of big business and
skyscrapers. Modern buildings are rising everywhere. With
its quickly growing population, Cairo is now building at the
rate of thirty-two houses a day.

When this writer crosses the Liberation Square, with its
huge 15-floor, 3000-room building, with the streams of cars
and fleets of buses flowing in all directions, with its lovely
fountain shooting its water several feet high, he remembers
some of his American friends in the United States who often
inquired whether camels and donkeys were the means of trans-
port in Cairo.

With its four universities and rich public libraries, Cairo is
a big cultural center. Perhaps it is the biggest in the whole East,

both Far and Near, and certainly the biggest in the Middle East. The University of Cairo enrolls 30,000 students (1958), Ein Shams University, 24,000, the ten-century-old Azhar University enrolls 5,000, and the American University about 1,000.

Cairo is also the Hollywood of the whole Middle East area. Egyptian films are extremely popular in the Arabic-speaking nations. Over one hundred films are produced each year by Cairo studios. The opera house in the winter season is rarely without some world-famous troupe. Indeed, the theater world in Cairo during the winter months is very active.

Sporting clubs are everywhere in Cairo. They are mostly in the suburbs or on the Gezira grounds (i.e. island between the banks of the Nile). Boxing, hockey, tennis, polo, golf, squash, swimming and football are common sports in those clubs. The Gezira Sporting Club is well known even to people abroad. Its membership exceeds ten thousand persons, and its area covers 30,000 square meters. It also has a large auditorium and a rich library. Besides such general clubs, there are a number of special ones, including the Automobile Club and the Yachting Club and many others.

Among all the cities of the world, Cairo stands alone as a cross section of human culture from its oldest days to its ultramodern phase.

10

AGRICULTURE AND THE COUNTRYSIDE

EGYPT HAS BEEN FOR MANY CENTURIES, AND WILL CONTINUE to be for a long time an agricultural country. Agriculture, therefore, is the cornerstone of Egypt's economy. Industry and commerce are determined by its products; and any attempt to raise the standard of living in Egypt must ultimately depend on its development. This is due to the fact that the vast majority of the Egyptians depend on agriculture to earn a living. About seventy-five per cent of the population live on land cultivation, and nearly two-thirds of the national wealth is invested in agriculture. And from agriculture sixty per cent of the annual income is derived. The land products form ninety-five per cent of Egypt's exports. More than half of the industry is based on the products of the land. In a word, to know Egypt is to get acquainted with the Egyptian farmer who is the pillar of its economy, and the basis of its social life.

The Arabic word "fellah" (plural: fellahin), which means the tiller of the land, is now often used as an English word to refer specifically to the Egyptian peasant. He is actually the backbone of the nation and the source of its strength. It is only fair to judge the Egyptian fellah by what he is, not by what he has. The economic standard of the fellah is low. The rapid increase in population combined with the limited area of the cultivatable land have seriously affected the standard of living of the villagers. But the have-nots of today may be in a better condition tomorrow. And vice versa. As we shall see later in this chapter, giant attempts are being made to raise the economic standard of the countryside. It is hoped that a radical change, in this respect, will soon take place.

In the fellah are deposited layers above layers of cultural legacy. If a geologist can tell the history of the world by digging in through the different strata of the earth's crust, a sociologist can tell much of the history of human culture by analyzing the character of the Egyptian fellah. Here you have the descendant of the pyramid-builder who never loses sight of the immortal life after death. Tempered by Christianity followed by Islam, he is an astonishing example of tolerance and love. A stranger may be suspected but never hated by him. One of the strangest traits of a villager's character is his suspiciousness of people's intentions toward him, together with an unshaken belief in divine justice. The small reward for continuous work on his farm all the year round, day in and day out, from sunrise to sundown, has never discouraged him. He loves his land and he loves to work on it.

Like all Egyptians, the Egyptian peasant is shy and sensitive. A keen sense of humor has always been his way of escape in the dark times. He is remarkably sociable. His intelligence is remarkably above the average. But his intelligence, charm and love of gaiety are often crushed by sickness and poverty. He is honest and likes to be honestly treated. An Egyptian peasant has every reason to be proud of his patience and dignity. He can suffer in silence as no other person can. But he never forgets maltreatment. Like a gathering storm he gathers his strength slowly but surely against despotism. Time and again have the villagers of Egypt produced the national hero who takes revenge for injustice. An invasion by one foreigner or the other, a phase of seeming quietude, and a national hero for redemption—this is the epitome of Egypt's history.

An Egyptian village is so different from a village in America that an Egyptian visiting the United States often wonders if there is in the States anything that may be called a village. A village in Egypt is usually composed of a few hundred houses closely gathered together in a mound-like shape. The streets are very narrow. Not a single square foot of land is left unused. The minimum of space is given to the dwelling area. Usually there is a main passage through the village, with all necessary shops. The minaret of the mosque always towers high above the mound of houses.

A villager's dwelling is very simple. It is generally built of mud-bricks, with low walls and small openings for windows. Fuel, such as dry cotton-sticks, is usually stored on the roof. Sometimes a shed is annexed to the house, where the farmer's animals and poultry are kept. In one of the rooms there is a built-in oven for baking bread. It is also used as a warming place in winter.

The peasant's food and clothing are extremely simple. Egyptians as a whole, and peasants in particular, are bread eaters. That is to say that bread forms a very big part of the meal. Lunch is almost invariably eaten in the field, not at home. It is always a cold and simple meal. A very common sight in the countryside at noon is that of the peasant's wife carrying lunch for the members of the family who work in the field. But dinner is always eaten at home. It must be a hot meal. Members of the family squat on the floor around a low table, usually with a round copper tray on it, and eat their evening meal in silence broken only with a few words now and then. This silence may be the result of a long day's labor. Or it may be due to a traditional respect for food, being considered as God's blessing. It is considered profane to treat food articles, especially bread, disrespectfully. Strong tea offered in glasses, and condensed coffee served in small cups, are about the only kinds of drinks used by Egyptian villagers. It will be remembered that alcoholic drinks are strictly forbidden by the Islamic faith.

The dress of the Egyptian peasant is even simpler than his food. The chief articles of his clothing are a kind of cotton garment (called *galabia*), some cotton pieces for underwear, a close-fitting cap made of either cotton or wool, and one or two coarse homespun articles made of rough wool for use in winter.

Something similar may be said about a peasant woman's dress: a couple of cotton dresses, one or two head-scarfs, a thin, black shawl, and a few cotton articles of underwear. She usually wears a necklace of big colored beads, an ordinary pair of earrings and a number of cheap bracelets. The Egyptian peasant woman is never veiled. There is no "harem" in the Egyptian countryside. Perhaps nowhere else in the world is there a more hardworking woman than the Egyptian peasant's wife. She spends most of her midday hours side by side with her husband right in the field. She is seen ploughing, harvesting and doing all sorts of agricultural jobs. She stays a little longer at home in the morning than her husband, to prepare lunch. And she goes back home a little earlier in the afternoon to cook the dinner.

It has already been said that Egypt entirely depends for the irrigation of its cultivatable land on the Nile. An elaborate system of dams and canals has been set up to irrigate as much land as possible on both sides of the river, and for as much of the year as possible. The water of the flood which comes in summer from the Abyssinian rains, is stored behind the Aswan Dam built at the farthest end to the south of the country. Every so often up the Nile stream, there is an auxiliary dam to raise the water level high enough to feed the canals running sideways. But the farmer has yet to use certain other devices for bringing the water from the local canal to his field. Simple implements are used for this purpose. They are the same implements that were used by his forefathers thousands of years ago.

First among these implements is the water wheel. A big wheel with hollow pockets on the sides of its rim is turned down a well by cattle or buffaloes. The pockets get filled when they are down, and emptied when they are up. Such a water wheel is called a *sakia*. It can irrigate from one to two acres of land per day. One can hardly think of the country-side in the still of the night without recalling the squeaking of the sakias pleasantly accompanied with a chorus of croaking frogs and sounding crickets.

Next to the water wheel in common use comes the *shadoof* —also an implement that goes back in history thousands of years. On a fixed post is supported a tilting pole, which can move up and down, with a large ball of dried mud at one end to serve as a lifting weight. At the other end of the pole there is a bucket tied to it with a piece of rope. A laborer stands below at the water level in the well or the canal. He pulls the pole down, gets the bucket filled, and then releases it. The weight at the other end of the pole automatically lifts the bucket up to the level of the field, where another man empties it into the minor trenches running through the farm.

Not only does the Egyptian farmer stick to his ancient predecessors' implements of irrigation, but also to other agricultural methods. He still ploughs his land with precisely the same machine that was used thousands of years ago. It consists of a pole about six feet long, drawn by an ox or any other beast of burden, attached to it at one end by means of a yoke. To the other end is fastened a piece of wood bent inwards and fitted with a sharp-edged piece of iron. For threshing the wheat, the farmer uses another ancient and simple machine. He uses a threshing-sledge which consists of a roughly made seat resting on a roller provided with sharp circular pieces of iron. The sledge is drawn by an ox, and it goes in a circle round the pile of wheat. The tiny pieces of the crushed stalks are stored in the farm barn for future use as food for the animals.

In addition to cotton, wheat and maize, Egypt yields a large variety of crops. Other cereals produced are rice and barley. Beans, lentils and peas are also grown in abundance. For textile materials, together with cotton, flax is raised. Chief among oil plants are sesame, earthnuts, castor-oil, and lettuce. Citrus fruits, grapes, pomegranates and melons are produced in large quantities. Sugar cane is planted on a large scale in Upper Egypt where big sugar refineries satisfy the local need. Among other vegetables, Egyptians grow onions, okra, pumpkins, cucumbers, eggplant, tomatoes, marrows, cabbage, radishes, turnips, potatoes, sweet potatoes, carrots, and beets.

The commonest tree to be seen in Egypt is the date palm. Dates ripen in August and September, at which time they show their variety of color in the fruiterers' shops. There are about thirty kinds of dates offered for sale. Next to the palm the acacia of the Nile (called the "sunt" tree) is most frequently seen by the wayside and in the country. The sycamore tree has been known for thousands of years, and was considered by the ancient Egyptians as sacred. The "lebbek" tree has been very recently introduced into the country to good effect. Within a few decades the lebbek tree attains a height of eighty feet and great thickness. Its branches extend to great distances, covering the roads with solid shade.

The general impression of the Egyptian countryside is of a checkered pattern of ribbed squares in different colors. The squares are bordered with water trenches and fringed with rows of trees, sometimes high sometimes low. Among the common colors in the fields are the deep green of clover, the gold-yellow of ripe wheat and the silver-white of the mature cotton. The crow, the ibis, the sparrow and the hoopoe and many other birds are on the green land or in the blue sky.

The fellah, even though the sinews of the nation, has been neglected and maltreated for hundreds of years. In most cases the rulers of the country cared for nothing except their own interest. The cultivated land was practically owned by a very small number of people leaving the rest of the population both landless and penniless. Although he was the actual tiller and cultivator of the land, the real source of Egypt's wealth, the backbone of its economy, the fellah could hardly obtain the bare necessities for existence. The economic and social scene in the village remained stagnant for ages and ages: a hardworking peasant miserably housed, fed and clothed. There would have been no hope for any real development of the country, had the conditions of the village remained as they were.

In 1952, drastic measures were taken. The maximum of land to be owned by one person was fixed at two hundred acres. Big landlords were thereby deprived of their undue power over the peasants working on their fields. The extra land, however, was not confiscated. Its possession was shifted to those who actually cultivated it. These new owners had to pay the price of whatever land they had thus acquired. Since they were penniless, the price was to be paid in installments spread over thirty years.

In 1961, land reform was further extended by reducing the maximum in land ownership from two hundred to one hundred acres. Furthermore, in order to raise agricultural productivity, measures have been taken towards consolidating small holdings into big efficient units.

Another of the most important measures recently taken for the social development of the village is the establishment of "rural centers." Such centers are designed to provide all the services required by the village. Each such center consists of a lecture hall equipped with a radio, a library, an outpatient clinic, an agricultural expert, a group of social advisers and visiting nurses and a number of instructors to teach the villagers home rural industries.

In each rural center there is a rural club, a playground and a model field, one acre in area, in which modern ways of cultivation are illustrated. Annexed to the center is a common cattle enclosure, a common trough for cattle, a pure drinking water system and a number of public baths.

The majority of illnesses throughout the villages is caused by infected drinking water directly drawn from the river or the local canals. The supply of pure and healthy water in the village, therefore, has been a most urgent necessity. Varied projects are now being carried out to meet the need.

In spite of all these reforms, the village as a whole looks unchanged. The most radical and most daring plan concerned with village reform has recently been blue printed. It is planned that all the age-old villages of the country should be replaced by brand new ones. It is calculated that such wholesale renewal is better than a patchwork of improvements.

The outline of the project is as follows. The building material is to be a scientifically formed mixture. Such mixture has been found to give the greatest possible strength at the lowest possible cost. A site in the neighborhood of each village (there are 4,000 villages in Egypt) is to be carefully chosen for the new construction. One experimental village has already been built in this fashion. The results seem encouraging.

Notwithstanding all that has been done lately toward the improvement of conditions in the countryside, Egypt's greatest problem has yet to be seriously met with and solved. The big question is: how to increase production in order to meet the rapidly increasing population? The fact is that Egypt's population is increasing at a rate not only in excess of the world average, but at a far greater rate than the ability of the present economy to sustain it. Egypt now has twenty-five million people, seventy-five per cent of whom live on six million acres of land. This cultivated area is already far from enough. What is going to happen a few years from now, if the population increases while the cultivated land remains as it is? One solution lies in industry. But agricultural production nonetheless, has to be increased.

Such increase is being heroically attempted both horizontally and vertically.

Vertically, the already cultivated land has to yield more than it actually does. The soil must be chemically more fertilized. Better species of different seeds have to be used. Losses caused by pests and insects should be brought to minimum. Livestock and poultry must be both improved and increased.

Horizontally, the area under cultivation must be expanded. Owing to the limitations of irrigation water, such expansion is no easy task. But attempts are being made to achieve such difficult tasks with every possible means.

The irrigation system has to be radically changed to save every possible drop of the Nile water, to meet the urgent need. A giant project is now under construction. It is considered one of the most gigantic projects in the world of irrigation. This is the High Dam project. The High Dam is being constructed about four miles to the south of the existing Aswan Dam. The new dam is planned to be about one thousand feet high, with a storage capacity of 130 billion cubic meters. Seven tunnels are being constructed on the eastern bank of the river for the discharge of its water. Four other tunnels are being built on the western bank to feed an underground electric power station. The dam itself, when completed, will be five thousand meters in length, and 1,300 meters in the width of its base. It consists of a big granite rock-fill block built across the river. President Nasser has rightly remarked: "For thousands of years the Great Pyramids of Egypt have been the foremost engineering marvels of the world. The pharaohs built them to ensure life after death. But tomorrow, the gigantic High Dam, more than seventeen times bigger than the pyramids, will provide a higher standard of living for all the Egyptians."

11

MODERN INDUSTRY

THE RAPID GROWTH OF INDUSTRY IN EGYPT TODAY STARTED during the First World War. There was a serious shortage of imported manufactured goods. Local industry had to cover such shortage. Several factories were established for various purposes. But as soon as the war was over, the imported goods poured in again, and the newly born local industry was in danger. In 1919, came a revolution that aimed at independence both politically and economically.

Before 1919, big business was mainly in the hands of foreigners. Most of the shares in banking and industry were owned by non-Egyptians. Such a state of affairs had to be radically changed, and soon. In 1920 an Egyptian bank was established. Misr Bank (Egypt's bank) appeared as a solid expression of the people's desire for economic independence. Apart from the usual banking activities, Misr Bank set itself to create and protect local industry. It created a large number of factories, covering a wide range of manufacture.

If Egyptian industry was born during the First World War, it was greatly stimulated by the Second World War. Again there was a considerable shortage of imported goods, and again local industry seized the chance to expand. Several new industries were created to meet the demand in such things as rubber goods and spare parts and tools. Industries, such as textiles and chemicals, already in existence expanded considerably.

Oil is the main source of power in Egypt. Local oil fields meet sixty-eight per cent of the demands of industry. The rest is imported. Egyptian oil fields are near the Red Sea. But the Western desert is now being searched with high hopes that new sources may be found. There are four pipelines, the longest of which is that from Suez to Cairo. Two major refineries exist in Egypt. The annual capacity of both is about 3 million tons.

At present the cotton textile industry is Egypt's most developed. About 150,000 workers are employed in the textile industry. The biggest center of cotton manufacturing is a city called El-Mahalla el-Kubra, right in the middle of the delta. The local output of cotton textiles meets the local demand. Imported material is now almost negligible.

Wool and silk materials are also locally made. Most of the local needs in silk, and about half the needs in wool, are supplied by homemade goods. During recent years, cotton yarn and some cotton fabrics began to figure in the export list of the country. The trend seems to be going substantially upward.

Together with the rapid advance of industry in Egypt goes an increase in the use of metals. Imports of iron and steel have been rapidly growing, and as a result the establishment of a local iron and steel industry has been initiated by three firms in 1949. The output has, however, been far from sufficient for the local needs. Early in 1958 a new big iron and steel mill, with a capacity of 220,000 tons a year, started to work. Raw iron is obtained near Aswan. Some parts of the desert have also been found to be rich in iron ore. Coal has to be imported. The increasing hydroelectric power, however, will gradually meet the fuel requirements. Accordingly some possibilities are opening up for a considerable expansion in the local output of iron and steel.

Fertilizer industry is vital in Egypt and is continually expanding to satisfy the ever-increasing demands of the farmers. A large factory in Suez has the capacity of 200,000 tons of calcium nitrate. A much larger factory has recently been established in Aswan which meets a sizable proportion of fertilizer consumption. It will use the hydroelectric power to produce 322,000 tons of nitro-chalk. Many other minor factories of chemical and organic fertilizers are located near the sources of power.

Enough other chemicals are also produced in Egypt to satisfy most of the country's needs. Soap, crude and refined alcohol, and perfume are manufactured in such quantities as to satisfy almost all the local requirements.

One of the most advanced industries in Egypt is the leather industry. About 2½ million pairs of shoes are manufactured annually. Nearly 36,000 workmen are employed in the trade. It is worth mentioning that a State factory sells shoes below their cost of production to the poorer classes. In general, leather products are of an excellent quality and their prices are remarkably lower than they are in other countries.

The world-famous Egyptian cigarettes are made in Egypt, but the raw tobacco is imported. Thirteen thousand workers are employed in the tobacco industry.

Sugar is crushed and refined in a huge factory, the third largest in the world. Candy and chocolate production uses up nearly one quarter of the total sugar output. Until recently Egypt exported its extra sugar. At present the local consumption has increased so rapidly that the whole output is used up internally.

The demand for building materials is enormous. Construction is going on everywhere. Old buildings are torn down to be replaced by new ones. Hundreds of semi-skyscrapers grow like mushrooms. As a result of all this the building industry is booming. Thousands of architects, builders and laborers are employed in this construction and reconstruction.

Concrete is among the most important of building materials. Since the basic materials for producing concrete are all found near Cairo, which is its main market, an enormous concrete industry has risen in the outskirts of the city. The industry consists of three firms, and employs some of the largest machinery in the world. Besides the concrete produced for building purposes, there is also a large output of concrete articles, such as pipes, telegraph and telephone posts, and cement tiles.

Egypt is passing through an industrial revolution. Until recently, the movement did not follow any set plan. There was no industrial policy in the country. In an effort to solve its economic problems, a planning board has been set up. It has the task of drafting plans and establishing priorities. The board is preparing an ambitious list of new plants: iron and steel, tires, jute, paper, electric cables, nails and tubes, among many others. The board has already implemented two successive plans for industrialization covering a wide range, with a special emphasis on engineering and heavy industry.

No less striking than the rapid industrial development is the social reform in the field of labor. After long neglect, the Egyptian worker has become, almost overnight, the grave concern of the Administration. It has been fully realized that laborers are the real sources of national power. No effort has been spared to create for them the best possible conditions.

According to the 1952 labor law, a worker is entitled to a vacation with full pay every so often. Certain favorable arrangements, both financial and medical, are made in cases of illness. Arbitration between labor and management has been set on a fair basis. Old age pensions are also arranged for. And for the first time in Egypt, farm laborers are given the status of "workers." They are now included in the laws governing labor-management relations.

The greatest advance, however, in the field of labor, took place in 1961 and after. Now workers are being converted into partners in most of the industrial concerns, with a share of profit and voice in management. In fact, the participation of the workers has gone beyond the field of business management. Workers, industrial as well as agricultural, account constitutionally for at least 50 per cent of the total seats of the national assembly.

12

EGYPT COMBATS ILLITERACY

WHAT EGYPT HAS DONE IN THE FIELD OF EDUCATION DURING the last quarter of a century is no less than a miracle. To be sure, sixty per cent of the nation, or even a little more than that, is still illiterate. But to estimate the achievement fairly, we have to recall the situation that existed until 1925.

When the British occupied the country in 1882, they took over the control of education among other things. But, it is tragic to say, the control of education in the hands of the British meant, for all intents and purposes, the check of growth. When the national revolution of 1919 forced them to loosen their grip, forty years after their occupation of the country, there were a dozen or so secondary schools and a small number of higher schools, but no secular university. There was no secondary education for girls at all, not to mention the university level.

Now look what has happened in the forty years' time during which the Egyptians have taken over the responsibility of their own education. There are 8,000 primary schools, 1,300 secondary schools, 200 of which are exclusively for girls. (A secondary school in Egypt is equivalent to senior high school in the United States.) Four large universities now exist, two in Cairo, one in Alexandria and one in Asyut. Twenty-three thousand female students attend various schools in these universities.

Nor was education under the British occupation defective in quantity alone. The type of education produced a certain kind of person: a submissive job-minded government worker. Schools were considered workshops to satisfy the demand of government offices. Students were taught just what was wanted for their future jobs, and non-creative jobs at that. The idea that all the people of the country should be educated, and for the mere sake of education, was not even dreamed of.

The poor quantity and quality of education naturally led to formation of two classes: the rulers on the one hand and the ruled on the other. Egypt was then known as the country where pashas ruled the fellahin—the former referring to the rich aristocracy, the latter to the poor, productive peasants. True democracy could never have been realized under such conditions.

When the Egyptians took over the control of education about forty years ago, they almost had to begin from scratch. Instead of being the right of the privileged alone, education was to become universal and free. All the children of the country, boys and girls equally, were given the right of a free primary education. It was even considered by law the duty of parents to send their children to school at a certain age. In other words, primary education was not only free for all, but also compulsory. At present 80 per cent of the children can find room in the elementary schools. It is expected that by 1970 the coverage will be complete.

The education system in Egypt today begins with what we call elementary school. It is free for all boys and girls between six and twelve to the capacity of the existent schools. A free midday meal is served for all. There is no distinction whatsoever at this stage. No fees of any kind are paid, and, consequently, no financial bar is raised before anybody. No consideration is given to any differences among people: differences of race, sex, color, class, or religion.

The six years covered by the elementary school, are divided into two units, four years for the first unit, and two years for the second. At the end of the first unit a written examination is held for all children. A final examination is held at the end of the six-year course.

Between the elementary stage and the secondary school is a three-year course called the preparatory school. Only those children who have attained a certain standard in the competitive examination are enrolled in the preparatory school. The selection is entirely based on merit. There is an equal opportunity open to all children with no discrimination.

The preparatory course, which extends from the ages of twelve to fifteen, leads to the secondary school. This is a three-year course, from the age of fifteen to the age of eighteen, during which the specialized study begins. There are two types of secondary school:

1. General secondary, laying the stress on theoretical studies.
2. Technical secondary, for vocational training in agriculture, industry or commerce.

The general type, with the emphasis on the theoretical studies, is chiefly to feed the various colleges. Students are classified, according to their abilities, into two main sections: one for humanities, and another for science and mathematics.

The specialization at this stage is, of course, not narrow. It is too early for an exclusive study of one subject. The two sections, therefore, have some subjects in common, such as the study of languages. However, it is at this point that the student decides on his future career. The graduates of the one section are admitted only to certain colleges, but not to others. A student of humanities, for instance, is entitled to enroll in the school of arts, but not in the school of engineering. The three-year course of the secondary school is ended with a secondary school certificate which is more or less equivalent to the high school diploma in the United States.

On the same level as the general secondary school, although with a different aim, stands the technical secondary school with its three subdivisions—agricultural, industrial and commercial. The aim here is to train a class of junior technicians in these different branches. It is a halfway house between the ordinary, unskilled worker, farmer or salesman, and the highly educated engineer, agriculturist or economist. By producing workers with such intermediate skills, the increasing demand for technicians is met.

Finishing the secondary course, a student is entitled to enroll in one of the universities or colleges. In most schools, it is a four-year course. In the schools of medicine, it is six-and-a-half-year course. Besides, there is a large number of post-graduate institutes for highly specialized studies. Every possible field of study is indeed covered in some school or the other. With a very few exceptions, the language of study is Arabic.

Such, in a broad outline, is the framework of the educational system. But over and above this formal system, there is a vigorously active informal campaign against illiteracy at all its levels. Since the compulsory elementary education, started in

1925, has missed the older generation, an effort is being made to form evening classes for the grown-up illiterates. Government departments and business firms that employ illiterate workers are responsible for the eradication of illiteracy each in its own sphere. Classes are open everywhere—in the armed forces, in the big firms, in jails for long-term prisoners, in social centers set up in the villages. In the years 1963–1964 so-called literacy units numbered 1,127, and catered to 114,212 men and women. It is expected that by 1980 illiteracy among adults will have totally disappeared.

Connected with this movement is an institute run by the Ministry of Culture called the People's Cultural Institute or sometimes just the People's University. This is mainly concerned with teaching adults who are already literate but would like to learn more. It only takes a group of people to show their desire to learn a particular subject or craft. A class is at once formed with that group. Thus the People's University caters to a large variety of tastes and needs. A number of housewives, say, may wish to learn dressmaking. A number of motorists may want to learn more about the engine. For any such group a course relevant to their desire is arranged. The People's University has branches all over the country, in almost every provincial city or town.

Also related to public culture, but in this case at a higher level, is a department whose concern is to encourage and raise the standard of public reading. Lest free-lance authors and translators omit certain aspects necessary for integrated culture, this government body sees to it that such gaps are filled. The aim in this respect is to keep the people up to date. Hence, recently published books in Europe and the United States are immediately translated into Arabic.

In a word, a full-fledged campaign is being waged in today's Egypt to combat illiteracy in all its forms.

13

WOMEN AND THE FAMILY LIFE

THERE IS, PERHAPS, NO OTHER ASPECT OF THE EGYPTIAN WAY of life that stirs the imagination of the people in the West more than the status of women. Whenever the question is raised, a strange picture readily jumps to the listener's mind. Veils, harems and polygamy are usually the chief components of such a picture. It is commonly supposed that Egyptian women live the kind of life portrayed in the *Arabian Nights*. A wife is always a member of a harem, locked in with other wives in the husband's house. She is thought to be barred from all public life, and if she dares to leave her home at all, she must be veiled. How romantic! But how untrue!

In fact the misconceptions about the status of women are often enlarged to include all women in the Moslem world. The imagined status is even supposed to be an essential part of the doctrine of Islam. This is far from true. Islam as such gives women a most liberal bill of rights. Hardly can there be a social right of which women are deprived on the basis of religion itself. According to the teachings of Islam a woman is fully responsible for herself both morally and legally. She has every right to possess her own property and to dispose of it without seeking the approval of any male guardian. She is allowed to keep her family name after marriage so that her per-

112

sonal independence should remain intact. She is entitled to enter any trade or profession.

Contrary to the widespread belief about the faith of Islam concerning women, their social position is elevated and their role as mothers is highly esteemed. Verse after verse in the Koran, the sacred book of the Moslems, defines the relationship between men and women as one of mutual confidence and mutual love. "The most perfect among the believers," said Mohammed, the Prophet of Islam, "are those who are kindest to their women-folk." He is also quoted as having said on a certain occasion, "Paradise lies at the feet of mothers," by which is meant that the path to Paradise lies in obeying and respecting one's mother.

Contrary, again, to the common belief, Islam did not order the seclusion of women. On many occasions in the recorded history of Moslem countries, women have risen to positions of leadership. They studied and taught in schools, traded in markets, and even fought on the battlefields.

When women in the Moslem countries have sometimes acquired certain traditions, such as veiling and a lower position in society than that of men, it was a sign of decadence rather than observance of religious doctrine. The veil, for instance, never existed in Arabia, where Islam first appeared. At that time no woman was ever veiled in Egypt. Pictures of women from all social strata, from queens down to laboring peasants, can be seen on the monuments of the ancient Egyptians. None of them is seen with a veil. It is not then the nature of the place, or the nature of the now-prevalent religion, that has brought veils in use. The veil was, in fact, introduced later in history as a mark of class distinction. It was originally used to distinguish the free from the slave. The slave girl alone was to be exposed to public gaze in market places. It will be observed that the veil was used by both Christians and Moslems in the Middle East. This distinction, however, concerned only the well-to-do classes. The peasant women of the villages and the women of the poorer classes in the city, were never veiled or secluded.

Egypt, it will be remembered, is an agricultural country. Over seventy-five per cent of the Egyptian women, therefore, are villagers. They work in the open fields side by side with their male partners or relatives. They are too busy earning their daily bread to think of a secluded life in a comfortable harem. With modern democracy and education, veils and seclusion have almost entirely disappeared even among the privileged classes. In the year 1923, in the heat of the national revolution, a distinguished feminist leader dramatically brought the matter to public attention. As she stepped out of the ship that brought her back from a women's conference in Rome, and in front of thousands of women and men who were there to welcome her home, she threw her veil into the waters of the Mediterranean. By so doing she publicly announced that the veil was no longer an accepted tradition. And thousands of women followed suit.

Education of girls in Egypt is little more than one generation old. But one generation of education has yielded wonderful results. Several hundred female doctors, lawyers, journalists and social workers are practicing their professions in the big cities. Several thousand female teachers are employed in schools of all stages. On the teaching staffs of the universities there are quite a few women scholars and professors in all branches of learning. Business firms and government offices employ thousands of women in various technical and ordinary jobs. Without any exception there is no discrimination between the sexes as regards wages and salaries and working conditions. The very Constitution of the country explicitly protects working women against any unfair treatment.

Far from being secluded in harems as they are imagined to be, they participate in all sorts of sport. They have even won championships, both national and international, in sports life: swimming, horseback riding, tennis and basketball. They have voting rights in the national elections. Dozens of women's societies are doing very good work in the social field.

The family life in Egypt is sound and healthy. Although polygamy is made legal by the Islamic doctrine under certain conditions, its practice in Egypt does not exceed three per cent of the married men. In spite of the fact that divorce is, in most cases, the right of the husband, the actual number of divorces is much smaller in proportion to the population than in many other countries. Perhaps this is due to the fact that women are sufficiently protected by religious laws against the abuse by men of their right to divorce. According to Islamic law, a man has to pay alimony to his divorced wife and their children. The alimony is estimated according to the man's income. The man who fails to pay the alimony in time is, according to the law, sentenced to jail. In Egyptian law, this is the only case where failure to pay a debt at the fixed time is punished by imprisonment.

Family ties in Egypt are too strong to be ignored. These ties are, in fact, a characteristic of agricultural people. It is a deeply rooted tradition in Egypt that family members should stick together. It is very common in the countryside to find, living in one house, a whole family with all its branches: parents, uncles, married sons and, sometimes, grandparents, too. In spite of the inconveniences created by such a large family living in one place, they still prefer it to breaking the family into small units. Foremost among the duties of a family member is to help a needy relative.

Here is a short description of how marriage takes place in Egypt. The following is a standard case.

Kamal is a schoolteacher. He is now a little over thirty years old. He was graduated ten years ago. His monthly salary is about thirty pounds (an Egyptian pound is worth 2.8 dollars). Ever since his graduation, he has been saving for his marriage. Much as he wanted to get married at an earlier date, he could not afford it.

His pay was still too small to support a family. Nor could he get married without a dowry. A bridegroom in Egypt has to pay his bride a certain amount of money as dowry. In the average case which we are describing, the required amount is something between six hundred and eight hundred dollars. In addition to this sum of money which is paid at the engagement, a smaller sum, about a half of the former, is to be included in the marriage contract as payable to the wife on a later occasion. Usually this latter portion is paid if the wife is divorced against her will. From the legal point of view, the dowry is the wife's own money. She can dispose of it in any way she likes. But in practice the rule is this: the bride's father pays as much as or even double or three times the dowry paid by the bridegroom. With the sum total an apartment is completely furnished for the married couple. The furniture is, of course, considered as the wife's property.

Now that Kamal is financially established, ready with the required dowry, he sets out to pick a bride. He does not happen to know any one who suits him. His relatives and friends learn of his wish to get married. Possible brides are, therefore, suggested to him. Amina, one of those mentioned seems to him a very good possibility. A meeting is arranged at a small tea party. The party may be given in the girl's parents' house, or it may be held in a public tea-shop. In the vast majority of cases, such a party is tactfully planned so that it assumes a casual atmosphere. Those arranging it see that there is the minimum of embarrassment. Kamal and Amina are thus given the chance to talk to each other. By the way, the would-be bride must not be less than sixteen years old. Eighteen years for the boy and sixteen years for the girl are fixed by the law as the minimum age for marriage.

Let us suppose that both Kamal and Amina, as a result of their meeting in the tea party, have decided to accept each other as future husband and wife. Such a decision soon comes to be known. Arrangements are now made in the girl's parents' house for a big party. It is the occasion for the bridegroom to offer his bride the engagement ring.

Usually the engagement is announced some time before the signing of marriage contract and wedding. Marriage procedure is considered as completed after the signing of the marriage contract. For this ceremony a big dinner party is given, usually accompanied by music and dancing. A government official, a turbaned sheikh, is invited to attend with his registers. Necessary forms are filled and signatures of both parties are secured. The moment it is known that the contract has been signed, the women of the party, utter shrieks of joy in a peculiarly traditional manner. Kamal and Amina are now husband and wife. At the end of the party, they go to their apartment which had already been prepared for them. Thus a new family is born.

14

SCIENCE, LITERATURE AND ART

EGYPT IS ARABIC-SPEAKING. ARABIC IS A SEMITIC LANGUAGE totally different from the Western group of languages. Hebrew may be the nearest to it. It is written from right to left. In its alphabet there are some letters the sounds of which have no equivalents in English, whereas almost all the sounds in the English alphabet are included. Hence it is more difficult for an English-speaking person to pronounce Arabic words than vice versa. There is, however, a wide difference between the classical Arabic which is used in writing and the colloquial dialects of everyday speech. The chief point of difference is that a number of terminal inflections in the former are dropped in the latter.

The Arabic language, with its subtle ways of derivation, is so rich and so easily adaptable that it now covers almost all details of modern science. Hundreds of Arabic textbooks on every subject are used by university students. To cope with the new requirements of ever-advancing science, the Academy of Language in Cairo, helped by various specialists, coins suitable words for every need. In case the original sources of the language fail to supply the adequate term, the Academy may transliterate the foreign term, maintaining the rules of pronunciation and word formation in the Arabic language.

A Higher Council for the Advancement of Science, together with a Research Council try to meet the local needs in the field of applied science. Many problems concerning local agriculture and industry are handled by these councils, sometimes with good result. Two prizes, 7,500 dollars each, are annually given by the State to the two most distinguished men of science. Together with these two big prizes, about ten smaller ones, 1,500 dollars each, are given to minor research workers in the field of science.

Similar prizes are yearly awarded to men of letters. Literature in Egypt, indeed the whole intellectual and cultural life, had long been in a state of stagnation until the middle of the nineteenth century. With the political awakening of the latter half of the last century, remarkable progress in the literary life began. Political struggle has given Egyptian literature its basic theme—Liberty. Liberty has been, directly or indirectly, the main subject matter of modern literature in Egypt, whatever the form and whoever the writer.

Important among the aspects of this liberating process is the struggle against the bondage of tradition, if such tradition proved deterrent to progress. A strong feminist movement during the last fifty years has been one of the big issues in the liberating activity of the writers.

Daily papers and other periodicals have been the most popular means of stirring the people to the new values of a new life. As a result, the "essay" type of literature has flourished. Until very recently, a writer in Egypt could hardly make himself known through books alone. Even a novelist would publish his novel in installments rather than wait till it appeared in book form.

The novel, however, is a form recently introduced into Egyptian literature. We exclude here such tales as the *Arabian Nights* which had only partly originated in Egypt. The publication of novels started in modern Egypt with an enormous number of translations from the West. It was soon observed that the novel was an attractive means of introducing history to the young generation. Numerous historical novels were published in the last decades of the nineteenth century and the first decades of the twentieth. The next development of the novel was centered on the peasant and rural life. This was the echo of the national revolution which flared up immediately after the First World War. The vast majority of present-day novels are still concentrated on the life of the toiling classes. This tendency is but a side issue of a more general characteristic of all Egyptian literature of today. Like any other literature written in the shadow of, or in the wake of political and social injustice, it is romantic. It lays more stress on the rural than on the urban aspects of life. It sympathizes with the poor, toiling classes against the sophisticated rich of big cities.

Curiously enough, when the ancient Arabs in the golden days of Islam (ninth and tenth centuries) translated into Arabic all the philosophy and science of the ancient Greeks, they deliberately refused to translate their literature. They were too proud of their own to import anything foreign. The result was that certain literary forms, including the drama, remained completely unknown in Arabic culture. It was only recently, not more than half a century ago, that we began to produce plays.

The drama in Egypt was born together with the stage. Hence we find that the actor, the producer and the playwright were all combined in one and the same man. The earliest plays were excellent as tools of social reform, but lacked much in artistic construction. The poor and lower middle classes were sympathetically pictured. The rich class was shown as morally dissipated and corrupt.

Early in its development, however, the drama took a great step forward. Plays in poetry were produced by gifted poets. Plays in prose with varying literary value are now being published in abundance.

But undoubtedly, the short story has been more successful in modern Egypt's literature than either the novel or the play. Dozens of young writers try their hand at this form of writing with excellent results. There is scarcely an aspect of our social life left unpictured in short stories. Nevertheless, short-story writers are chiefly preoccupied with the life of the peasants and the working class of the city. Their themes are taken from everyday life of ordinary people. The features of their life, their work and amusements, their joys and sorrows are realistically described. They faithfully hold the mirror up to the nature and society of modern Egypt.

Arabic literature throughout all its history had been remarkably rich in poetry, especially lyric poetry. Poetry had been almost the only fine art in which the Arabs excelled. This was due to the fact that words were the only artistic material at hand. The nomadic forefathers, on the backs of their moving caravans, could sing to the steps of their camels, but could not sculpture or paint. These latter arts require settlement, and the desert nomads were always on the move.

Nevertheless, with all that rich legacy in poetry, modern Egyptian poetry has undergone a big change. It has been deeply influenced by the impact of the West in modern times. The form of the poem has changed considerably. The unity of the poem was something hardly known to a classical poet. An ancient poem was composed of brilliant beads lacking the string of unity to make them a necklace. But our contemporary poets have now learned that a work of art should have an organic unity.

More important still than the artistic unity in the revival of poetry is the sincerity of feeling among our contemporary poets. It so happened during the last century, and long before that, that poetry had lamentably deteriorated to something artificial and dead. The poet, then, would versify for other reasons than to express his private experience truly and sincerely. He would compose his poem to show his linguistic ability or to praise a man of importance in the hope of a reward. Nothing short of a revolution would have sufficed to change the whole attitude within the poet himself. A genuine poet, indeed a genuine artist, should regard nothing beyond his own feelings. And this is a noticeable feature of modern Egyptian poetry.

Besides creative literature in its various genres, there has been developing since the middle of the nineteenth century a very large body of translations into Arabic from other languages. Five hundred translated books, at the least, are published every year. Apart from individual efforts, the movement is sponsored on a large scale by certain official and semi-official bodies. A Higher Council of Literature and Art, among its various efforts to encourage all aspects of literary production, encourages the translation movement with ample rewards for translators.

In fact, not a single art in Egypt is now without a radical revival. The traditional school of music is losing ground, and the progressive trend is gaining. In painting, the contemporary artists include representatives of all the modern trends. Architecture has departed completely from the old decorated villa to the semi-skyscrapers. Artists and men of letters have actually torn the medieval cobwebs off the face of Egypt, and brought her into the modern world.

INDEX

Abdu, Mohammed, 73, 74
Abukir, 66
Agriculture, 15, 73, 91-100
Aida, 70
Akhenaton, 27-29
Al-Afghani, 73
Al-Azhar University, 51
Alexander, 21, 22, 23, 32, 79
Alexandria, 21, 32 34, 55, 68, 73, 79-82
Al-Hazen (Ibn Al-Haytham), 57
Allah, 41, 42
Allahu, Akbar, 44
Alphabet, 29, 119
Al-Qahira (Cairo), founding of, 50
Amon, temple of, 32, 55
Amr Ibn el-Aas, 69
Apostle, Age of, 34
Arab League, 78
Arabi, Ahmed, 71-73
Arabia, 40
Arabian Nights, 55, 60
Arabic Language, 41, 109, 119
Architecture, 17, 27, 55-57, 124
Area of Egypt, 12
Art, 17, 20, 30, 31, 56; Contemporary, 122-124; Early Egyptian, 80, 83; Greco-Roman, 80
Ashura, 52
Aswan, 14; dam, 95, 100-103
Aurelius, Marcus, 79
Ayoubids, 53, 54

Babylon, 33, 34
Bank, Misr, 101
Bread, 37
Breasted, James Henry, 26, 27
British rule and interests, 66, 76, 78, 106

Caesar, Julius, 33, 79
Cairo, 16, 21, 23, 33, 44, 50, 55, 56, 58, 77, 78, 82-90
Calendar, 16, 29, 42
Caliph in Bagdad, 49

Camera obscura, 57
Canals, Alexandria, 81; Red Sea to Mediterranean, early, 26; Suez, 29, 66-73, 76, 78
Champollion, 30
Christ, 33, 34
Church of Egypt, 34
Cigarettes, 103
Citadel of the Rams, 86
Civilization, four types of, 22
Cleopatra, 33, 80, 81
Climate, 16, 17
Commerce, 15
Concrete, 104
Constantinople, 65
Coptic Church, 38
Cotton, 68, 73, 96, 102
Cretans, House of the, 86
Crops, 96
Crusades, 52, 53

Dams, 68, 73, 95, 100, 102, 103
Darius, 29, 69
Day of Judgment, 43
de Lesseps, Ferdinand, 68, 69, 73
Deserts, 16
Diocletian, 80
Discrimination, religious, 38, 39
Dowry, 116
Dynasties, 22, 23

Education, 106-111, 114
El-Malhalla el-Kubra, 102
Euclid, 79

Falouga, 76, 77
Family life, 112-118
Farouk, King, 77
Fatima, 52
Fatimids, 50-52
Fellah, fellahin, 67, 92-100
Fertilizer industry, 103
Folklore, 60-64

French rule and interests in Egypt, 66, 74, 78

Galabria, 94
Gawhar, 50, 51
Geographic characteristics, general, 11-18
Geographical Society, 82
Giza, 17, 20, 24, 83
Greco-Roman Period, 32, 55

Hannibal, 33
Harem, 112, 114
Hatshepsut, Queen, 27
Heliopolis, temple of, 33
Herodotus, 24, 26
High Dam, 100
Holy Family, 33
Hussein, 52
Hyksos, 23
Hymn to Aton, 28

Industry, 101-105
Iron, 102, 103
Irrigation, 68, 95, 96, 100
Isis, 14
Islam, 38-49, 56-58, 75, 112, 113; rituals of, 44, 45
Ismail, 70, 71
Israel, 76, 78

Jerusalem, 34, 45
Joseph, 26
Judaism, 42, 47

Kamil, Mustafa, 75
Karnak, temple, 26, 27
Kephren, 83
Khamsin, 18
Khan el Khalili, 84, 85
Khartoum, 13, 14, 67
Khufu, 23
Kleber, 66
Koran, 40-44, 46, 47, 113

Labor-Management Relations, 104, 105
Languages, 22, 109, 119
Language, Academy of, 119
Law, effects of Nile floods on, 15, 16

Leather, 103
Liberation Square, 89
Libraries, burning of, 79; value of, 26
Libya, 12
Literature, *Arabian Nights*, 60-64; early, 20; Higher Council of Literature and Art, 123; modern, 120-124
Luxor (Thebes), 55

Mameluks, 54, 65, 66
Marriage, 116, 117
Matarieh, 33
Mecca, 40, 41, 45, 67
Medina, 41, 67
Memphis, 16, 21, 22
Mena, 16, 21, 22
Middle Kingdom, 23, 26
Mohammed, 40-43, 46, 47, 52, 113
Mohammed Ali, 66-68
Mohammedanism, *see* Islam
Monastery, of St. Anthony, 37
Mongol, barbarians, 54
Moslem, *see* Islam
Mosques, 44, 55, 56; of Cairo, 56, 85, 86
Mousky, 84, 85
Muezzin, 44, 45, 56
Myths, legends, 14, 86, 87

Napoleon, 49, 51, 65, 66, 81
Nasser, Gamal Abdel el, 77, 100
Nationalism, 71-77
Necho, King, 29, 69
Nefertiti, Queen, 27
Nelson, 81
New Kingdom, 23, 26
Nile, 11-19, 37, 68; Blue Nile, 13; White Nile, 13

Obelisks, 27
Oil, 102
Old Kingdom, 23
Origen, 35, 36
Ottoman, invasion, 54, 58
Ox, 12

Pagans, Roman, 34, 36
Palestine war, 76-78
Papyrus, 26

People's Cultural Institute, 110
Persians, conquest by, 29
Pharaohs, 21-31, 82
Pharos, 79
Philo, 79
Plotinus, 79
Polygamy, 115
Pompey's Pillar, 80
Population, 12, 81, 82, 89, 99
Power, hydroelectric, 102, 103
Printing press, 66
Prophet, see Mohammed
Ptolemies, 32, 33
Pyramids, 15, 100; Battle of, 66; of Cheops, 23; of Giza, 17, 20, 24, 83

Railways, 82
Ramadan, 46, 47
Rameses II, 27
Religious, 20; Akhenaton, first believer in one God, 27-29; Christianity, 21, 22, 32-39, 47, 79; Islam (Mohammedanism), 22, 38-49
Revolutionary Command, 78
River engineering, 15
Roman rule of Egypt, 33
Rural Centers, 98

Sa'id, 68
Saints: Anthony, 21, 36-38; Mark, 34, 35, 80; Peter, 34
Sakia, 95
Saladin, 53, 85
Sale, George, 41
Scholars, 57
Schools, 81, 106-109
Science, 20, 120
Scott, Sir Walter, Talisman, 53
Scribe, Statue of, 83, 94
Second Intermediate Period, 23
Senusert III, 26

Shadoof, 95
Sheikh, 51, 52
Shipbuilding, 15
Siti I, 69
Siwa, oasis of, 32
Slaves, see Mameluks
Sphinx, 23, 25, 86
Sports, 81, 90, 115
Steel, 102, 103
Stephenson, George and Robert, 82
Sudan, 12, 67, 73
Suez canal, see Canals
Sugar, 103
Sultan Hassan, mosque of, 56

Taxes, 45, 46
Tewfik, 71
Textiles, 102
Theater, Cairo, 90
Thebes (Luxor), 26; temple of, 27
Thutmose III, 27
Touloun, Ibn, 86
Trees, 96, 97
Turkish rule and interests, 65, 71, 72
Tutankhamoun, 27, 84

Ulysses, 79
United Arab Republic, 77, 78
Universities, 81, 90, 106, 109; People's, 110

Veils, 113, 114
Verdi, 70

Wahhabites, 67
Women, 112-118
World War I, 75, 101; II, 76, 101

Zaghlul, Saad, 75
Zuheir, 58